THE WAR ON FREEDOM AND DEMOCRACY

The War on Freedom and Democracy

Essays on
Civil Liberties in Europe

Edited by Tony Bunyan

Spokesman Books
for the
European Civil Liberties Network

European Civil Liberties Network (ECLN)
contact: info@ecln.org
website: http://www.ecln.org

The ECLN does not have a corporate view nor does it seek to create one. The views expressed are those of the author.

© ECLN 2005

First published in 2006 by
Spokesman Books
Russell House, Bulwell Lane
Nottingham NG6 0BT
England
Phone 0115 9708318   Fax: 0115 9420433
e-mail: elfeuro@compuserve.com
www.spokesmanbooks.com

ISBN 0 85124 723 7
ISBN 13 978 085124 723 6

A CIP Catalogue is available from the British Library.

Printed by the Russell Press Ltd., (phone 0115 9784505)

CONTENTS

Introduction

These Essays were prepared for the launch of the European Civil Liberties Network (ECLN) in October 2005. The passage of time since then has served to emphasise the relevance of the issues raised and the analyses provided.

Five years have now passed since 11 September 2001. The war on the so-called 'axis of evil' has been exposed as an unmitigated disaster. But the 'war on terrorism' continues with no end in sight, insidiously permeating the institutions of the body politic, sacrificing liberty and freedoms in the name of a constructed 'politics of fear' and the demands for security.

We have learnt that the greatest threat to 'our way of life' and democracy comes not from terrorism but from our governments' reactions to it.

The emergency measures that at first were presented as 'exceptional' are now the norm. European Union leaders say that measures adopted (or proposed) 'balance' the demands of security and civil liberties.[1] They are needed, we are told, to protect 'our way of life' and the 'core values' of the European Union.[2]

If the swathe of measures brought forward in response to 11 September 2001 represent the 'core values' of the European Union then I, together with many others, say 'Not in my name'.

It was with these developments in mind that we sat down to see if a wider network could be created to link struggles across Europe. The Network's founding statement says:

'We are living at a moment in history when civil liberties and democracy are under attack as never before and the need for a collective response to counter these threats has never been greater.

We share common objectives of seeking to create a European society based on freedom and equality, of fundamental civil liberties and personal and political freedoms, of free movement and freedom of information, and equal rights for minorities. This entails defending, extending and deepening the democratic culture – a concept not limited to political parties and elections but embracing wider values of pluralism, diversity and tolerance. And we share too a common opposition to racism, fascism, sexism and homophobia.

The defence of civil liberties and democracy also requires that positive demands are placed on the agenda. For example, respect and rights for all people, cultures and their histories, for the presumption of innocence and freedom from surveillance and the freedom to protest and demonstrate.'[3]

Many thanks go to Spokesman Books for publishing the collection and especially Tony Simpson for all his work. Thanks to those who took time to prepare their essays and to Trevor Hemmings who subbed and cleaned-up many of the contributions. Our gratitude goes to Courtenay Griffith of Garden Court Chambers who spoke at the ECLN launch in Brussels, and to the European Federation of Journalists and Ann Singleton, Katrin McGauran and Yasha Maccanico who helped make the launch so successful.

Tony Bunyan
October 2006

Footnotes

1 The Statewatch 'Scoreboard' published in March 2004 showed that of 57 proposed measures 27 had little or nothing to do with tackling terrorism.

2 See innumerable speeches by Mr Solana and Commissioner Frattini.

3 ECLN website: http://www.ecln.org

1

'The rules of the game'?

A. Sivanandan

We live in such a vortex of change that no sooner have we seized the time than it has passed us by. But that is the very reason why we must be more vigilant than ever about constraining power and invigilating the insidious ways the government has to change 'the rules of the game'. To do that, however, we need the courage to abandon old ideologies which bear us down, the honesty to turn our faces against intellectual fads and fetishes, which turn us away from engagement, and the commitment to fight injustice wherever we find it. We also need the type of political analysis that Owen and Godwin, Saint-Simon and Fourier, Marx and Engels did for their time in the maelstrom of the industrial revolution – an analysis immanent in which were the strategies that would inform the working-class struggles against capital – and out of that conflict elicit, if not socialism, at least the democratic rights and freedoms that have come down to us.

And it is those rights and freedoms that we are in danger of losing today. The working-class forces that won them for us have been disaggregated and dispersed by the technological revolution – even as that revolution concentrates wealth in the hands of giant corporations and sets them free to roam the world, the nation-states of the West clearing capital's imperial way by setting up stooge governments for consenting Third World countries, and regime change for those who refuse to play imperial ball. National governments, which under industrial capitalism worked in the interests of their people, under electronic capitalism work in the interests of multinational corporations – and the welfare state concedes to the market state, where those who own the media 'own' the votes that elect the government, where the social fall-out is mediated through welfare sops and controlled through draconian legislation which corrodes the whole fabric of civil society.

Some of these processes were already there in the very nature of globalisation. The fall of Communism hastened them and made them universal. September 11th entrenched them, and the ensuing war on terror added a *military* dimension to the *economic* project justified through a *politics* of prejudice and fear to create a *culture* of xeno-

1

racism and Islamaphobia: the asylum seeker at the gate and the shadow Muslim within.

It is that symbiosis between racism and imperialism, and imperialism and globalisation that now frames our times. We cannot combat the one without combating the others. Imperialism is the project, globalisation the process, culture the vehicle, and the nation-state the political and military agent. To look at racism as an isolate without considering its relationship to globalisation, and therefore imperialism, is not only to descend into culturalism and ethnicism but to overlook the state racism that embeds institutional racism and gives a fillip to popular racism in the form of laws and edicts that starve and dehumanise asylum seekers whom globalisation has displaced and thrown up on the shores of Europe.

To look at globalisation without relating it to imperialism and therefore racism is not only to regard its penetration into Third World countries as an inevitable extension of trade, not as a precursor to the regime change that follows in its wake, but to overlook the racist discourse that accompanies it and in turn feeds into popular racism.

To look at imperialism without relating it to globalisation and racism is not just to accept the notion that regime change and pre-emptive strikes have no underlying economic motive, but have a defensive strategy against 'the axis of evil' and the terrorists they breed – ('post-modern imperialism', Robert Cooper, one-time adviser to our PM and the EU, calls it). It is also to accept the hoary old myth of the white man's burden of bringing civilisation and enlightenment to the lesser breeds, of freeing them from tyranny, forcing them to be free, bombing them into freedom and democracy. Except that the underlying theme this time is not that of a superior race but of a superior civilisation. Hence the real war, not the phoney war, is not between civilisations, as Huntington would have it, but against the enforced hegemony of Western civilisation.

To put it another way – under global capitalism, the relationship between the economic, political, cultural etc., is so organic that we can no longer think of society in terms of superstructure and base, with the economic base determining the political and cultural superstructure. That would have done for industrial capitalism. But electronic capitalism requires us to think in terms of circuits, not hierarchies. And the dynamo that drives those circuits is the free-market system.

The market, in its turn, dismantles the public sector, privatises the infrastructure and determines social need. It violates the earth, contaminates the air and silts up the rivers. It creates a two-thirds, one-third society of the have-everythings and the have-nothings, and keeps poverty from the public gaze. It reduces personal relationships to a cash nexus (conducted in the language of the bazaar) even as it elevates consumerism to the heights of Cartesian philosophy: I consume, therefore I am.

The irony is that when our rulers ask us *sub-homines* to live up to their values, it is not the values they exhibit that they refer to, but those of the Enlightenment which they have betrayed. Whereas we, the *sub-homines*, in our very struggle for basic human rights, not only hold up human values, but challenge Europe to return to them. We are the litmus test of western values. The Enlightenment project is incomplete till its remit of liberty, equality and fraternity is extended to the non-white peoples of the world. That is the challenge that our presence in Europe signifies.

Nor is the task of the Reformation over – so long as there is a connection between Church and State (as in Britain) – which in practice privileges the state religion over all others. That, again, is the challenge that Islam, Hinduism, Sikhism etc present.

On the other hand, states that pretend to secularism, like France, are still to distinguish between rites and rights. The religious symbols that people exhibit (like the cross and the hijab) may in their view be a rite but, from the view of the secularist state, it is a right. For what, in the final analysis, defines a secular state is the paramount importance of individual liberty: my freedom is only limited by yours.

September 11th and the war on terror have given the British government the excuse to develop a new virulent strain of anti-Muslim racism to go hand in hand with the punitive laws against asylum seekers – till all of us 'Others' are, at first sight, terrorists or illegals. We wear our passports on our faces or, lacking them, we are faceless.

However, since July 7th, the London bombings, anyone whose face is not quite the right shade, who does not walk in exactly the right way, who does not wear the right clothes for the season, can be taken as a potential suicide bomber – as law-abiding Brazilian electrician Jean Charles de Menezes learnt to his cost. And, if you're recognisably Muslim (or just believed to be Muslim), you will be subject to official stops and searches by the police and to unofficial racial attacks and harassment in the community.

July 7th has also signalled a more dangerous tendency on the part of the executive to make incursions into the preserve of the legislature. A case in point is the administrative powers the Home Secretary has arrogated to himself through changes in existing immigration laws – to deport anyone suspected of 'unacceptable behaviour', even to countries that accept torture on the basis of 'memoranda of understanding' that these particular deportees will not be tortured! These are powers that, in effect, complement and reinforce anti-terrorist legislation – but by side-lining parliament and public debate. And the more the executive arrogates more and more power to itself (it is after all the Home Secretary and not the courts who decides who will be detained, who will be subject to control orders and who will be returned to face torture) and expects the judiciary merely to rubber-stamp its decisions, the more the role of the judiciary and the respect in which it is held is undermined. Besides, the separation of powers, which silently characterises Britain's unwritten constitution and is therefore the more to be cherished and safe-guarded, is being systematically undone.

Blair's reasoning behind all this is that July 7th has changed 'the rules of the game'. But the game is democracy and not one part of it can be changed without starting a chain reaction that unravels the whole.

A Sivanandan is Director of the Institute of Race Relations and Co-editor of 'Race and Class'.

The 'war on terror': lessons from Ireland

Paddy Hillyard

Marx made many comments about history. But one particular comment is important when reflecting upon the current war on terror. He pointed out that history repeats itself, first as tragedy and second as farce. This is an apt description for the current racheting-up of the anti-terror legislation by the United Kingdom parliament. It conveniently ignores the 105 'Acts of Coercion' in Ireland in the nineteenth century, which did little to quell the dissent and led eventually to the granting of independence. It tragically ignores the Special Powers Act, the Northern Ireland (Emergency Provisions) Acts and the Prevention of Terrorism Acts of the twentieth century. Most of these anti-terrorist measures were counterproductive. Many of the actions taken simply served to increase the levels of violence and alienation and prolonged the conflict before a political settlement, rather than a military defeat, could be obtained. Now history repeats itself as farce.

The new terror laws include outlawing 'glorification' of terrorism, an offence of acts preparatory to terrorism, laws against giving or receiving terror training, a law against the indirect incitement of terrorism, laws against bookshops selling extremist material, the reintroduction of internment in the guise of detention with suspects able to be held for up to a month, and the requirement that those applying for British citizenship must be of good character. Many of these measures have been tried before in some form in Ireland. The aim of this short paper is to comment on some of the more important measures.

Internment

The single most disastrous measure in Northern Ireland was the introduction of internment in 1971.[1] Symbolically, it suggested to the nationalist population that their demands for a more fair and just society in Northern Ireland could no longer be carried forward through dialogue and persuasion. The rule of law had been abandoned. Nearly 2,000 people were interned over the period and less than 150 of them were Protestants. Practically, it led to hundreds of young men in working class nationalist communities joining the IRA and creating one of the most efficient insurgency forces in the world.

Torture

Internment was accompanied by the 'torture' of a selected number of internees. It involved the use of five techniques. Each internee was spread-eagled some distance from a wall and made to place their hands against the wall to hold their weight. A hood was placed over their heads and a high-pitched whine was played. If they fell down they were beaten and placed again in the same position. They were deprived of food and sleep. The government set up a Committee of Inquiry to investigate the allegations under Sir Edward Compton.[2] He was not asked to comment on the legality of the techniques and made a vacuous distinction between 'brutality' and 'physical ill-treatment', deciding that the techniques fell into the latter rather than the former category. The confirmation that the techniques had been used and the attempt to argue that the practices did not amount to brutality united the Catholic community behind the IRA. In 1975 Amnesty established an independent Commission and reported on a number of further cases of ill-treatment of prisoners and internees.[3] The revelations further alienated nationalist communities.

When the images began to emerge from Abu Ghraib prison showing prisoners hooded, humiliated and tortured few people in Northern Ireland were surprised and expressed deep cynicism when the authorities claimed that the practices were not systemic but the unauthorised behaviour of a few individuals. The lesson from Northern Ireland is that these barbarian methods of interrogation were common practice within the British Army and no doubt within other armies worldwide and approved at the highest level. To compound matters, the government now appears to be prepared to allow evidence obtained through torture in other countries to be admissible in criminal courts in Britain. All of this barbarism is supported by a number of academics justifying torture on the grounds of the greater good.

Shoot-to-kill

The shooting dead in London of Jean Charles de Menezes, the innocent Brazilian going about his daily work, has drawn attention yet again to the use of lethal force by police officers. The contrast in thinking about the issue in Britain and West Belfast was neatly captured by the headlines in two newspapers. *The Sun* carried the headline; 'One down and two to go' while *Daily Ireland* carried the stark headline 'Executed'.

For years there were allegations that there was a 'shoot-to-kill' policy particularly targeted on the IRA and other Republicans. It was always denied. Stalker (then Assistant Chief Constable of Greater Manchester Police), who investigated the deaths of six young men at the hands of the RUC in the 1980s pointed out in a letter to *The Times*: 'I never did find evidence of a shoot-to-kill policy as such'. However, he then went on to say that 'there was a clear understanding on the part of the men whose job it was to pull the trigger that that was what was expected of them'.[4] In other words, there was a policy but Stalker was not allowed to see the evidence for it. Moreover, it has long been suspected that the security services colluded with loyalist paramilitaries in the assassination of republicans. The report by Judge Cory into the murder of Pat Finucane provides prima facie evidence that this was indeed the case.[5] It therefore came as no great surprise when it was revealed following the shooting of Menezes that a shoot-to-kill policy for suicide bombers had been introduced and disseminated to all police forces by the Association of Chief Police Officers without informing either parliament or the public.

Stop and search

Early in the conflict, the powers of stop and search, arrest and detention were extended throughout the United Kingdom. Again there is ample evidence of the counter-productive nature of these developments.[6] Thousands of innocent people experienced humiliating situations on the streets, at ports and airports and in detention facilities. Very few were subsequently charged as a result of the arbitrary use of the powers and those that were charged were not charged with terrorist but with ordinary criminal offences. These powers created 'suspect communities' within Northern Ireland and, more importantly, a 'suspect community' in Britain.[7] Anyone who was Irish, or had a connection with Ireland or had Irish relatives and friends, became a suspect. Sometimes it was simply an accent, looks or passport that gave rise to suspicion in the minds of the public or the police.

The problem with arbitrary and draconian police powers is that they alienate the very communities from which the police require good intelligence. People are not going to report incidents or crucial information to the police when either their last contact has been at best unpleasant and at worst humiliating and abusive or they have heard how a neighbour or relative has been treated. Good intelligence is essential to prevent acts of terror, yet the authorities still appear to lack an understanding of the crucial role of good police community relations in this endeavour.

Banning freedom of expression
The policies developed to deal with Irish political violence included measures directed at specific organisations. Various organisations were banned and new criminal offences were introduced, such as being a member of a proscribed organisation or collecting money for the organisation. In addition, a broadcasting ban was introduced to prevent members of illegal organisations speaking on radio or TV. These policies did little or nothing to destroy the organisations. On the contrary, they were pushed into greater secrecy and the broadcasting ban, which prevented open and political discussion of their aims and objectives, further retarded a political rather than a military solution to the problem.

The arrest and conviction in September 2005 of the Syrian born journalist Taysir Alouni in Spain on the grounds that he had collaborated with members of Al-Qaeda has worrying parallels with the attempt in Northern Ireland to prevent the freedom of the press. It will have a very negative impact on reporting worldwide and make it even more difficult for the public to obtain a non-western perspective on events in Muslim countries. One of the key pieces of evidence used against Alouni was that he had taken $4,000 to Mohammed Bahaiah, an Al-Qaeda leader. He denied that he knew that Bahaiah was an Al-Qaeda leader and he argued that he carried the money as an act of Muslim good manners. As he put it: 'I took it, and that is not a bad thing ... If you refuse you are looked upon badly. What is more, I was interested in these people because of the information that I needed.'[8]

The use and possible misreading of cultural expectations to secure convictions also occurred in the notorious 'Birmingham Six' miscarriage of justice case. The six had planned to go to the funeral of James McDade, who had blown himself up in a bomb attack. The fact that the six planned to go to his funeral in Belfast was exploited by the prosecution to suggest IRA connections and sympathies rather than a strong Irish cultural practice of respecting the dead even where the person is not particularly well known to the mourners.

8

Transformation of the ordinary criminal justice system

The criminal justice system in Northern Ireland was radically transformed in order, it was argued, to deal more effectively with those suspected of political violence.[9] Juries were abolished and the rules of evidence were substantially changed with limitations on the right to silence and a lowering of the burden of proof. At the same time, a range of different strategies were used in different periods in the conflict to obtain evidence; ranging from the use of brutal interrogation techniques[10] to the widespread use of supergrasses[11] and informers. In effect, there were two criminal justice systems operating in Northern Ireland: one for those suspected of terrorist activities and another for those suspected of 'ordinary decent crime'.

The development of a separate criminal justice system to deal with political violence has corrupted the ordinary criminal justice process in three significant ways. First, powers and procedures, for example, relating to the length of detention under anti-terrorist legislation were subsequently incorporated into the ordinary criminal law. Secondly, anti-terrorism legislation was constantly used to deal with ordinary criminal behaviour. Thirdly, the whole criminal justice system became discredited as the rule of law was replaced by political expediency and the Northern Ireland judiciary did little to uphold the independence of the law.

Accountability

Another major lesson to be learned from the Irish experience is that all organisations involved in dealing with political violence, from the secret services to the units handling public order on the streets, must be independently and democratically accountable. The last thirty years in Northern Ireland is strewn with examples of organisations and agencies acting beyond the law or else mobilising the law for their own political ends.[12] These range from the brutal methods of interrogation, through the 'Bloody Sunday' debacle, to widespread collusion between the security services and paramilitary killers.

Conclusions

The lessons from Ireland are clear. Widespread violation of human rights in the so-called 'war against terrorism' is counterproductive. It erodes democracy by undermining the very principles on which social order is based and alienates the communities from whom the authorities need support in dealing with political violence. Moreover, it is vital that those involved in dealing with political violence must be independently accountable to democratic scrutiny and the rule of law. The threat from political violence is real, as witnessed in Bali, Madrid, Washington, New York, London, Kabul, Basra or Baghdad. But we must avoid at all costs inflaming the passions that lead people to become involved in political violence. This makes it even more imperative that those in power do not abandon the rule of law and the prevention of terrorism becomes, as it did in Ireland, the terror of prevention.

Paddy Hillyard is Professor of Sociology at Queen's University Belfast. His book Suspect Community: People's Experience of the Prevention of Terrorism Acts in Britain *(Pluto, 1993) is still the only ethnographic study in Britain of the impact of anti-terror legislation on people's lives.*

Footnotes

1. See McGuffin, J. (1973) *Internment* (Tralee, Co Kerry: Anvil Press).
2. Report, C. (1971) *Report of the Enquiry into Allegations against the Security Forces of Physical Brutality in Northern Ireland arising out of the Events on 9th August 1971* (London: HMSO).
3. International, A. (1975) *Report of an Inquiry into Allegations of Ill-Treatment in Northern Ireland* (London: Amnesty International).
4. *The Times*, 14 February, 1988
5. See; Cory Collusion Inquiry Report: Pat Finucane, HC. 470, HMSO, 2004. http://www.nio.gov.uk/cory_collusion_inquiry_report_(with_appendices)_pat_finucane.pdf
6. See for example: Boyle, K., Hadden, T. and Hillyard, P. (1975) *Law and State: the case of Northern Ireland* (London: Martin Robertson) and Hadden, T., Boyle, K. and Hillyard, P. (1990) *Ten Years on in Northern Ireland* (Cobden Trust: London).
7. Hillyard, P. (1993) *Suspect Community: People's Experience of the Prevention of Terrorism Acts in Britain* (London: Pluto Press).
8. See 'When a reporter got too close to the story, *The Media Guardian*, 3 October, 2005.
9. Commission, D. (1972) *Report of the Commission to Consider Legal Procedures to Deal with Terrorist Activities in Northern Ireland* (London: HMSO).
10. For brutal police methods see: Taylor, P. (1980) *Beating the Terrorists? Interrogation in Omagh, Gough and Castlereagh* (Harmondsworth: Penguin).
11. Greer, S. (1995) *Supergrasses: A Study in Anti-Terrorist Law Enforcement in Northern Ireland* (London: Clarendon Press).
12. See fore example, Ní Aoláin, F. (2000) *The Politics of Force: Conflict Management and State Violence in Northern Ireland* (Belfast: Blackstaff Press).

3

Why terror and tolerance are the greatest test of modern journalism

Aidan White

There is no greater challenge to journalism today than finding words and images that help us to understand the nature of terrorism and religious fanaticism without falling into the trap of negative media coverage of Arab and Muslim communities.

Anti-Arab intolerance is on the rise, as is anti-Muslim sentiment, and Western media stereotypes of the Arab world seem to be greater and more dangerous than they have been for decades. Too often media fail to distinguish between fundamentalism and mainstream Islam and appear to regard engagement with religious communities as forever compromising to progressive values.

In the process, there is another story – one of heroism and the struggle for rights – in the Muslim world which is being missed altogether. If ever there was a need for good, honest reporting and for facts to be placed in the context of social change it is now, but there is little evidence that media are rising to the challenge.

Of course, the emphasis on terrorism and fanaticism in the Arab world has been made worse by the war on terrorism. It is an obsession, fed by sensationalist and superficial reporting of conflict in the Middle East and nurtured by unscrupulous and racist politicians. It contributes to an increasingly fearful climate within previously stable metropolitan communities in Europe and the United States.

Today in countries with a history of tolerance like Norway, Denmark, Belgium, Austria and the Netherlands, a toxic cocktail of prejudice and ignorance about Arab culture is leading to a resurgence of extremist politics not seen for 50 years.

Europeans are waking up to a difficult reality – that immigrants who began coming to Europe in the 1950s when governments and businesses encouraged mass migration, are profoundly alienated from European society and remain unreconciled to their situation in Europe. Some have turned to the most grotesque interpretation of the Islamic faith to give their lives meaning and there is a growing attachment to violence on the fringes of the diaspora.

The multicultural dream of Europe is being eclipsed everywhere.

But no one, apart from the die-hard racists, are able to describe what will replace it. The danger is that the anti-Muslim discourse of Jean-Marie Le Pen's National Front in France or the Vlaams Belaang Party in Belgium or the British National Party may become part of the political mainstream.

The decline of investigative and thoughtful journalism is partly to blame. Even worse, some media have turned their backs on European models of balance and impartiality which are essential to the quality of this debate and complex discussion.

The murder of film-maker Theo van Gogh by a lone Muslim extremist in Amsterdam, for instance, unleashed a spiral of Islamophobia, in which Dutch media, previously standard bearers for tolerant reporting, did little to dampen the fires. The government considered closing mosques that spread 'non-Dutch values.' Primary schools for Arab children were fire-bombed. Attacks on Muslim and Arab communities increased. In Britain, the same pattern of racist violence against Muslims followed in the wake of the London bombings of July 2005.

Media responses have often reflected a profound uncertainty, mirroring the political paralysis and drift to extremism that threatens fundamental rights and stability within society.

Yet a return to the basic building blocks of good reporting – asking simple questions, putting facts in context and striving for balance in comment – may well provide a solution.

Are Muslims really a threat? In Europe, for instance, the number of people voting for openly xenophobic parties in most countries exceeds the number of Muslims let alone those who inhabit tiny cells of Islamic extremism. In truth, Europe poses a far greater threat to Muslims than Muslims do to Europe, but this reality hardly figures in media coverage.

Who is harassing who? Countries with minority Muslim populations devote increasing police resources and efforts to the monitoring of Arab and Islamic communities. The number of Asian people stopped and searched in the UK, for instance, increased by 285% in 2002/3, fuelling resentment in already alienated communities.

Under the banner of 'radicalism and recruitment', Muslim communities' places of education and worship across Europe are being targeted for increased surveillance. Racial profiling, a practice theoretically prohibited by international law, has also made a come back. There have been renewed arguments about wearing 'the veil' at school and about use of religious symbols, all of which have added to the tension.

Are Islamic countries fomenting 'extremist' societies? A climate of suspicion and press scaremongering, bolstered by some absurd notions of a 'clash of civilisations,' is contributing to support and electoral success for anti-immigration and far-right political parties. Yet no one who visits the Middle East can believe that communication is now controlled by governments or that society relies on traditional voices or the Mosque.

Radical changes in every aspect of the forces that shape public opinion, such as the yearning for social justice, free expression and fundamental rights, are an ongoing reality in much of the Middle East and North Africa, despite the presence of outdated laws and, in some quarters, a still unreconstructed and corrupt political class.

In fact, change is in the air and the evidence is to be found in the invigorated newsrooms of Arab media like *Al-Jazeera*.

Arab states are singular and complex. They are vastly different, both in economic and cultural traditions. Many do operate in a political and social climate where secular political options attract a limited following, but the reasons are rarely fully explained.

In the routine stereotype of Western media, Islamic extremists on the margins of society are confused with the whole Arab world; Arabs are typecast as supporters of terrorism and in the background is a growing media fixation on a millennial clash between Islam and Christianity.

But burning resentments in the Arab world, much of them focused for decades on the injustice of the conflict in Palestine, are too complex to be reduced to such simple terms.

Even limited research by reporters of political rebellions against Western domination in the region would reveal they have been mainly secular. Arab nationalism, though often associated with Islam, is sometimes at odds with it. Pan-Arabism, some of whose founders were Christians, offered an alternative, more secular, form of cohesion even if it was not necessarily more democratic.

Its failure and Western interventions, often imperialist in nature, leading to the toppling of freely-elected governments and the support of dictators, have not helped the cause of democratic change, but may instead have contributed to a revival of Islamist movements.

Although Western media tend to suppose that the lack of separation between church and state is the basis for Islamist

13

revolutions, they ignore the fact that in the non-Arab Muslim world, in places like Indonesia and Malaysia, religious ideologues have failed to make much headway.

Indeed, more pragmatic Muslims in many countries are keen to separate politics from religion. They form a significant body of opinion in the ongoing debate in the Muslim world on Islam and democracy and Islam and modernity. This inner conflict rarely surfaces in Western media coverage.

Despite all of this, the rhetoric now building in both the West and the Arab World is of a final showdown between great religions. Social democratic governments are moving further to the right, abandoning the ideals of diversity and pluralism.

The time may be right for a new dialogue between western and Arab world media professionals about rights and tolerance in journalism. We may also think it is the right time to revive anti-racist campaigning within journalism to counter xenophobia which was a feature of cross-border co-operation among journalists' unions in Europe during the 1990s.

Journalists and media need to navigate through these treacherous developments with some sense of professionalism. If they do not, then the onward march of intolerance and racism, with its bleak and pitiless inhumanity, can be guaranteed.

Aidan White is Secretary-General of the European Federation of Journalists.

14

4

While Europe sleeps ...

*Under the 'war on terrorism' a veneer of democracy is
legitimating the creation of a coercive (and surveillance) state*

Tony Bunyan

I. The context

Five years on we know that the 'war on terrorism' is going to be
permanent, not temporary.[1] This is not just because of 11 March 2004
(Madrid), 7 and 21 July 2005 (London) and terrible terrorist
bombings elsewhere. It is also because the pre-conditions for further
attacks persist and show no signs of abating – Iraq, Afghanistan,
Palestine, US militarism, Guantanamo Bay, rendition and global free
market economics which perpetuate poverty and gross inequality.

The 'war on terrorism' is going to be permanent for another
reason. There are major differences between the USA and the
European Union (EU) over the war against the 'axis of evil' – Iraq,
Iran and North Korea. However, there are few, if any, differences
between them over the 'war on terrorism' – apart from ones of style.
As to content we have seen the creation of a EU-US 'axis' on matters
of tackling terrorism, money-laundering, organised crime, and crime
in general not just at home but globally.[2]

The permanence of the 'war on terrorism' means that new
repressive laws and powers given to the security and intelligence
community and the law enforcement agencies (LEAs) cannot be seen
as exceptional and time limited to meet a temporary crisis. In
combination they change the relationship between the state and
individual and, in turn, constitute the new norm.

The 'war on terrorism' (and the 'politics of fear' based on the clash
of civilisation and barbarism) serves another, deeper, purpose. For a
brief period the 'Cold War' and globalisation, which emerged as the
new global economic system in the early 1980s co-existed. But with
the end of the Cold War in 1989 globalism (the ideology of
globalisation) lacked a political ideology to legitimate itself. This
gap left globalism exposed as the raw, aggressive, exploitative,
capitalism that it is – where tackling poverty and disease will always be
secondary to the maintenance and advancement of western standards
of living.

15

The 'war on terrorism' was a god-send (and not just in George Bush's conversation with the Almighty). Globalisation, the economic, now had a legitimating, political, ideology. This is why, if for no other reason and there are many, the 'war on terrorism' is with us for the foreseeable future.

The differences and similarities between the Cold War and the 'war on terrorism'

There are a few similarities but many differences between the Cold War era and the 'war on terrorism'.

Between 1945-1989 there were several competing ideologies. To name a few, there was capitalism and 'liberal-democracy' in the West, Soviet-style state communism, Chinese communism, and many different kinds of socialism in the Third World. Today there are no competing ideologies which makes the 'war on terrorism' all the more pervasive and dangerous because it is on its way to becoming hegemonic.

A Sivanandan described this moment in *Race and Class*:

> *'Globalisation has set up a monolithic economic system. 11 September threatens to engender a monolithic political culture, if they come together they spell the end of civil society'.*[3]

He is not arguing that civil society will disappear, simply that critical alternatives – whether in the media, trade unions, academia or the NGO/voluntary sector – will become marginalised (or criminalised).

Another difference between the Cold War era and the present one is that in the latter there was a very real threat that nuclear war could indeed have destroyed 'our way of life' and our 'democracies'. However, the terrorism we are now witnessing in Europe is terrible and horrific but it will not destroy 'our way of life'. What will destroy 'our way of life' and 'democracies' is the reaction of governments and the EU to terrorism.

There is yet another difference. In the era of the Cold War the West espoused 'liberal-democracy', which as an idea included representative democracy (political parties, elections and parliaments) and a political culture of tolerance, diversity and pluralism. It also, in Western Europe, extended to the welfare state, state-run industries for the essentials of life (like water, electricity and gas, and transport) and even the notion of the redistribution of wealth to help the poor.[4] Of course it only partially, and in some areas never, delivered but as an idea it marked the high-water mark for 'democracy' and liberal values. Today it is bereft of almost everything but a shallow 'representative democracy'.[5]

In Europe 'representative democracy' is the norm where principles have given way to pragmatism, and the retention of power is the primary aim of the main political parties.[6] This shallow form of democracy (centred around elections and not a democratic culture) combined, since 2001, with its authoritarian direction leaves us with the veneer of democracy masking the creation of the coercive (and surveillance) state.

II. A 'gulf of understanding'

There is in the EU what can be called a 'gulf of understanding' between its institutions, national governments and officials and critical civil society. Since 11 September 2001 we have been looking at the same world events through different eyes and have come to utterly different conclusions.

So when the EU speaks of 'core values' and/or 'shared values' – as if referring to a consensual response to threats, like terrorism – what are these values and have they changed?[7]

Are the values of the late 1990s, when they were 12 broadly social-democratic governments and three on the right (the EU then had 15 member states), the same as today when there are five on the so-called centre-left (including the UK government) and 20 on the centre-right or extreme right?

Certainly I would have to say that if the polices and practices in reaction to terrorism since 11 September express these 'shared values' then they are not ones that I, and many others, share.

For example, EU institutions and national governments claim that all the measures introduced and planned *balance* the demands for security and the rights and liberties of the individual – and what is frightening is that they actually believe this.

In 2004, Mr Vittorino, previous Commissioner for Justice and Home Affairs, and in 2005, Mr Solana, Secretary-General of the Council of the European Union (representing the 25 governments), said in answer to critics of the responses to terrorism that:

'Our way of life has not changed'[8]

To which can be asked:

'Whose way of life has not changed, the lives of white Europeans?'

17

Life changed dramatically for refugees, asylum-seekers and third country nationals resident in the EU. Laws and rights were changed to exclude whole categories from applying for asylum, applications for asylum fast-tracked and legal advice by lawyers curtailed by cutting back on their fees, detention centres mushroomed across Europe, 'voluntary' repatriation (expulsion) is backed by forcible expulsion in chains, countries never considered 'safe' before were declared 'safe' to send people back to[9], hundreds have died trying to cross the Mediterranean or end up dead on Europe's beaches and increasingly sophisticated technology is employed to track and seek out people fleeing from persecution and poverty.[10]

All refugees have come to be viewed by the EU as potential terrorists, and if not terrorists then potential criminals.

Third world people legally resident or citizens of the EU, especially Muslim communities, have became the target for 'stop and search' on the street (where police often cannot distinguish between 'muslims' and 'third-world-looking people') and raids of community centres and homes.

In the autumn of 2001 the German government proposed that each state should set up a database of all resident third country nationals in the EU. At the time this was rejected by the other EU governments as going too far – only Germany and Luxembourg had such registers. In 2003 the EU agreed that all third country nationals resident in the EU should be fingerprinted and given a biometric card (with the fingerprint data on a chip) and the details held, initially, on a national database.[11]

Life for third country nationals granted the right of residence has changed in another way too. Now country after country is insisting that this (and the granting of citizenship) is dependent on migrants and their families learning the host country language and 'integrating' into its society. As Europe, imbued by the 'politics of fear', moves from multiculturalism to monoculturalism third world peoples are expected to adopt the values of the host country above their own histories and culture.

In the UK people granted citizenship now have to attend an official ceremony swearing allegiance to the Queen – as subjects not citizens – and sing 'God Save the Queen'. There are millions of British people who would refuse to do this, me included.

It can only be described as wilful deception to suggest that 'our way of life' has not changed – for it is to say that we, the people of Europe

– are not responsible for what is being done in our name to everyone who is not a white European.

But even this assessment is too generous.

Since 11 September the EU has embarked on a series of measures which it would never have dared bring in during the Cold War era – some of which have not even been proposed in the USA.

III. How the landscape of the EU is changing
The surveillance of telecommunications

First, there is the mandatory retention of all telecommunications traffic data – phone calls, e-mails, faxes, mobile phone calls (including location at the time of the call) and internet usage. That is the details of all communications by everyone present in the EU.

Perhaps the least of our concerns is that we are all going to end up paying for the cost of being put under surveillance (whether through increased charges or state subsidies).

Of greater concern is how that data is going to be used. The security and intelligence agencies (and usually the police) already have access to this data when targeting a 'suspect', where a specific person is under investigation the powers already exist to intercept their communications and view/read the contents of them.

In the UK the agencies have daily access to reams of data collected by Government Communications Headquarters (GCHQ) and its global network (shared with the National Security Agency in the USA).[12]

So if security and intelligence agencies can already get access to the data for the purpose of combating terrorism why is the new measure being proposed? It is argued that the hundreds of law enforcement agencies (LEAs) in the EU need the data to combat terrorism (and a lot more) – *but nowhere do you see in any EU document that these powers are needed by the national security and intelligence agencies.*

The great danger is that access to traffic danger will be used by the law enforcement agencies to go on 'fishing expeditions' during what is called the 'investigative' stage (ie: prior to there being any concrete evidence to pursue a criminal investigation that could lead to charges and trial). The danger too is that traffic data (and other 'intelligence' on file) gathered by an agency in Country 'A' is passed to another in Country 'B' which adds further 'intelligence' before passing the file on to Country 'C' (which may be outside the EU).[13]

There is nothing in the European Commission's proposal on data protection for police and judicial cooperation which would stop this scenario happening everyday.[14] Such exchanges would simply require the agreement of the 'owner' (the agencies not the individuals) of the personal data, an agency in Country 'A', to pass over the information and 'intelligence' (which may be correct or simply supposition) to Country 'B' and agree it can be passed on to Country 'C' (which could be a non-EU state like the USA). The process will be 'self-regulated' by the agencies and not subject to direct scrutiny by external bodies (eg: data protection authorities). The person on whom the intelligence is held has no right to be told of the transaction nor to what further uses it is put (unless, of course, they are brought to trial).

The surveillance of movement

Second, the EU agreed in April 2004 to introduce checks on all movements in and out of the EU by air – with its very own 'passenger name record' (PNR) system. This followed the highly controversial EU-US agreement to allow the USA access to all PNR details for those flying there. At the moment this data (and many suspect that for other destinations) is extracted from the airlines computer reservations system operated by companies like Amadeus.[15]

In the UK it is not possible to book a flight online with British Airways for an internal flight (eg: London to Aberdeen) without agreeing that the PNR data can be passed to the USA.[16]

The EU-US passenger name record agreement is being challenged in the European Court of Justice by the European Parliament. The primary concerns, voiced inside and outside the parliament, were over the adequacy of data protection in the USA (where its Privacy Act only gives rights to its own citizens) and how many and which US agencies would have access – questions the US government could not answer.

In the USA itself there was a major debate over collecting passenger information and how it would be used. CAPPS II was the original system which was going to check all passenger data against a host of state and private databases to catch suspected terrorists and criminals, to exclude 'undesirables' and build up 'profiles'. This was until the General Accountability Office (GAO) report which failed CAPPS II on seven out of eight privacy and data protection criteria – from that point on the scheme was dead.[17] In place of CAPPS II is 'Secure Flight' which will carry out much more limited checks against a suspected terrorist list of around 125,000.[18] At least it can be said that the US

'Secure Flight' list appears to be limited to suspected terrorists, whether EU and national lists will be similarly limited is not known.

The EU passenger name record scheme, when the 'technical details' are agreed, will track the movement by air of everyone in and out including that of EU citizens and resident third country nationals.

Once in place PNR databases will be used not just to record who enters and leaves but under the 'Advanced Passenger Information System' (APIS) will put all passengers into one of three categories: Green, you can board. Yellow, subject to extra checks of baggage and person and/or questioned or placed under surveillance on arrival. Red, placed under arrest on arrival at the airport or at the check-in desk. Of course there are flaws in this system, tests have shown that between 5-15% of passengers can be classified as 'yellow' depending on whether a narrow (terrorist suspects) list is used or a wide (terrorist, organised crime and any crime) list. And the biggest flaw of all is that if the intelligence and security agencies do not know that a person is a terrorist then they will simply get on the plane through the 'green' channel.

Visa Information System
For visitors to the EU the Visa Information System (VIS) is being set up. The plan is that all visitors will have to have their fingerprints taken (all 10 of them) and this biometric data is inserted on a 'chip' in the visa to be put in their passport. Finger-prints will usually be taken at an EU member state mission in their home countries. Personal details and the biometric will be put on national and then the EU-wide VIS database.

The database is being built to cope with 100 million records dealing with 10 million visa-holders a year. As a number will be regular visitors it is estimated that in the first ten years a total of 70 million records and sets of fingerprints will be held. This is a very ambitious project as it will be the biggest finger-print database in the world (currently the largest is the FBI's with 45 million records). Moreover, a feasibility study on the Visa Information System in 2003 pointed out the difficulties that could occur as the size of the database grows – that the error rate increases and with the size of the database and this could not be quantified.[19]

Another major, and as yet unresolved, issue arose in the autumn of 2004.[20] There will be a 'clash' of 'chips' if the non-EU passport issuing countries opted for biometric passports themselves. The visa chip would 'kill' the passport chip rendering both unusable.

Whether the non-EU states will object to having an EU biometric visa inserted into its passports is not known.[21]

To make a start the EU has selected a number of target countries (including Russia and China) to start a dual process covering visas and the EU demand for the automatic re-admission of people who have come from that country and that EU states want to deport back to them. The tactic is one of blackmail – called 'Visa facilitation and readmission'. The EU will agree to 'facilitate' issuing visas to a country's citizens in return for agreement on re-admission. The aim is for:

'a visa-free travel regime as a long-term perspective.'

In the so-called 'visa dialogue' with third countries the 'carrot' is to offer moving that country to the 'white-list' of countries (for whom visas are not required, like the USA and Japan) from the 'black-list' (countries whose people need a visa – which in future will require the taking of their finger-prints). They are reminded of the:

'Relevant factors to be taken into account in any discussion on the transfer of a third country from the black list to the white list'

To the wholesale surveillance of telecommunications and of movement can be added the wholesale surveillance of everyday activities of everyone resident in the EU through biometric documents.

The onset of biometrics

The decision of the EU to introduce 'biometric' passports was taken in December 2005.[22] It was argued that the EU needed to respond to international demands for 'biometric' travel documents in line with the adopted standard of the International Civil Aviation Organisation (ICAO) – a move emanating in G8 led by the USA and the UK. However, the ICAO standard is only for a digital picture of a person to be included – this is simply the normal passport picture sent in with a postal application being 'digitised' and the image inserted into a 'chip' which can be read. This allows 'one-to-one' checks at the points of entry and departure that the person carrying the passport is the same person as on the digitised picture.

It provides for a very basic check and has been erroneously referred to by government ministers and officials as the introduction of 'biometric passports'.

The biometric passport measure adopted in the EU is going to involve the taking of two fingerprints from everyone applying for a new passport (or for the first time). As many people living in the Schengen area (12 EU countries plus Norway, Iceland and Switzerland) travel within these countries using their ID cards there is a proposal under the Hague Programme to set 'minimum standards' for ID cards – which no doubt will 'harmonise' the use of fingerprints on them.

The UK has not 'opted-in' to the Schengen provisions on border controls and immigration and is thus not covered by the EU scheme – which is why it is proposing to introduce its own 'biometric passports' (this leaves Ireland which also has not 'opted-in' to decide what to do). The UK is introducing biometric passports from the autumn of 2006 (for first-time applicants) and then for all renewals. This will involve the taking of fingerprints and a facial scan (a scan plotting and storing up to 1,840 unique features on a person's face) and maybe even a 'iris scan' as well.

Biometrics and the personal details of the individual will initially be stored on national databases and later be brought together on an EU-wide database.

The implications of this move are enormous. Over the next ten years as passports are renewed millions of people will have to physically go to a 'processing centre' to be 'enrolled'. In the UK the estimated number is over 5 million people a year. 'Enrolment' will involve not just having to go to a centre – instead of putting an application in the post – when there people will be interviewed and have to present documents to prove who they are. Then the biometrics will be, compulsorily, taken.

In the UK everyone issued with a new passport (whether renewed or first time) will automatically be issued with an ID card as well.

People living in the Schengen area (28 countries) who have ID cards will be subject to the same processes when the new measure is adopted.[23]

Biometrics and surveillance
When the whole picture is put together we are heading for a Europe where:
● all visitors with visas will have been finger-printed and will be tracked in and out, and an historic record of each visit will be held (a bit like the US-VISIT programme) for future reference;

● all resident third country nationals will be finger-printed and issued will a biometric card; their movements in and out will be tracked;
● all EU passport-holders will be fingerprinted from 2007 onwards;
● all ID cards will also include fingerprints – travel in the Schengen area is usually carried out with ID cards;
    to which can be added, in the longer-term,
● biometrics on driving licences;
● health cards with biometrics and personal medical record on the 'chip'[24].

When biometrics become the norm pressure will grow from companies to have access to the data, for example, to know the health record of a potential employee or before giving insurance.

I do not believe most people in the EU realise what is happening and that they will have to:
● compulsorily present themselves in person at an 'enrolment centre'[25];
● be 'interviewed' to prove they are who they say they are;
● to compulsorily have their fingerprints taken (and a 'facial scan' too in the UK which will log 1,840 unique features of their face).

We are heading for a Europe where in time – with bank and credit cards added – everyone will have one card containing a myriad of personal details that will have to be presented to establish 'identity', to get access to everyday services and buildings.

As national databases give way to EU databases, which are 'interoperable' (as those who inhabit the institutions talk) or when there are 'synergies' between the databases, then the 'principle of availability' will pave the way to a nightmare society.

Under plans for 'interoperability' 'synergies' are to be created between Schengen Information System II (SIS II), the Visa Information System (VIS), the Customs Information System (CIS) and Eurodac (holding all the finger-prints of asylum-seekers) including fingerprints and DNA – passenger name records will no doubt be added when the EU has decided how to set it up.

The creation of biometric databases is going to start in 2007/8 and because passports and ID cards are generally issued for ten years the process will not be complete until at least 2018.

The rationale (and claimed legitimation) for the creation of the world's largest collection of personal biometric data is the 'war on terrorism', the need to trade privacy and rights for security. In security and intelligence terms this argument is nonsense. By 2012, at the earliest, only 50% of people in the EU will be covered and 50% will not which is not much use if 50% of the suspected terrorists (and those who are not suspected) get through or can move around undetected.

The 'principle of availability'
The EU governments in the Council of the European Union are preparing a proposal, under the 'principle of availability', for law enforcement agencies (police, customs and immigration) to exchange information and intelligence – including DNA – held by them. Secret, but unpublished, documents show that their plans go much further. Law enforcement agencies should:

> *'have direct access to the national administrative systems of all Member States (eg: registers on persons, including legal persons, vehicles, firearms, identity documents and driving licences, as well as aviation and maritime registers'*[26]

A later document elaborates on this. Law enforcement agencies in the EU should exchange information and intelligence not only held ('owned') by them but also 'information held in databases not owned' by them in other state databases (eg: vehicles) and:

> *'information held in private databases (eg: a telephone numbers database owned by a telecom company) but which is **available** to law enforcement authorities'* [emphasis in original][27]

The draft definition of 'information and intelligence' to be exchanged within the EU (and outside) is defined as that held by the agencies and:

> *'any type of information or data which is held by public authorities or by private entities and which is **available** to law enforcement agencies without the taking of coercive measures'* (emphasis in original, op.cit)[28]

Under these mechanisms for wholesale surveillance everyone becomes a 'suspect'. The 'principle of availability' will mean, in time, that if there is anything 'suspicious' the state will know. And the mass of personal data gathered will be marginal in tackling terrorism. It is like building an ever higher haystack while trying to find the same number of needles – replacing targeted intelligence-gathering with a great mass of innocent 'chatter' may indeed hinder rather than help stopping terrorist attacks.

According to an unpublished overview report on this 'principle' EU citizens want 'freedom, security and justice' but:

> *'It is not relevant to them [citizens] how the competencies are divided (and information distributed) between the different authorities to achieve that result'*[29]

25

The EU is heading down the road where the law enforcement agencies will have access to masses of personal and intimate data without any data protection worth the name.

IV. What is the rationale and who are the forces behind these developments?

A few of these proposals were around before 11 September 2001 but were 'on hold' either because other EU governments thought they were a step too far or due to sustained pressure from civil society (eg: over mandatory data retention).

The 'war on terrorism' changed the rules of the game. Now, the argument goes, there is a continuum running from terrorism to money-laundering (though this primarily concerns organised crime and drugs, not terrorism), organised crime, serious crime and all crime. After all, one European Commission report argued the methodology is often the same as all use mobile phones – but does this make everyone who has a mobile phone a 'suspect'?

The Commission report on exchanging information on terrorist offences argued for bringing together the:

> 'Union's arsenal of weapons against terrorism. Many of these are not specifically anti-terrorism but range wider while including terrorism [and] a link should be established between terrorism and other forms of crime [even though these are] not immediately obvious... If the fight against terrorism is to be totally effective, it must be handled in conjunction with the fight against other forms of crime'.[30]

Many of the measures agreed or planned have no place in a democracy worthy of the name and result from a *confusion of aims* – is the aim to tackle terrorism or something quite different? After the dreadful attacks in Madrid on 11 March 2004 the EU re-vamped its Action Plan on terrorism. Statewatch examined these and concluded that 27 of the 57 measures had little or nothing to do with tackling terrorism.[31] At the time we commented:

> 'Under the guise of tackling terrorism the EU is planning to bring in a swathe of measures to do with crime and the surveillance of the whole population. After the dreadful loss of life in Madrid we need a response that unites Europe rather than divides it'.

It is consistently argued that the 'law enforcement agencies' need all these measures to fight 'terrorism'. There are many flaws in this argument. First, on the front-line in combating terrorism are the intelligence and security agencies not the law enforcement agencies.

It is they who collect SIGINT (signals intelligence), COMINT (communications intelligence), OSINT (open source intelligence) and HUMINT (human intelligence) – though the latter was significantly run down prior to 11 September 2001 as the old 'enemies' of the Cold War were no more and the new ones not clear.[32] In most countries these agencies have all the powers they need. While the law enforcement agencies, in respect of terrorism, play a secondary and supporting role.

Combating 'terrorism' has, and is, used by governments, officials, the law enforcement agencies keen to extend their powers, status and budgets, even if their role is secondary.

The other vested interest is that of the multinationals who are going to make billions out of the new technological demands of wholesale surveillance. Once established in Europe (and the USA) these new standards will become the benchmark for 'global standards' (and even more billions of profit).

A classic instance of the state-multinational interface at the EU level was the setting up of the 'Group of Personalities' in the autumn of 2003. This was set up, met in secret, and reported back without any consultation with parliaments or public. It was comprised of 30 people, one-third from the Council and Commission, one-third from big 'research' organisations and one-third from multinationals.[33] Its final report laid down the need for a 'European Security Research Agenda', for which billions of euros should (and are going to be) allocated. Among its proposals are the creation of a military-civil interface (with vetted experts and academics), the creation of a 'military-industrial complex' to compete with the USA, and the production of tracking devices for vehicles, goods and people.

When faced by terrorism governments ask for solutions. The form and specificity of many of the 'solutions' offered is a combination of the long-standing demands of the law enforcement agencies and the technological 'fix' offered by multinationals seeking to create and exploit new, global, long-term markets. The decision-making process is mediated by high-ranking officials in national Home/Interior Ministries, the General Secretariat of the Council and their counterparts in the USA and G8.

V. The EU state and the state of democracy in the EU
Some academic theorists discount the idea that a European state is under construction largely because their theories are based on the

development of the 'first pillar' (the economic and social) of the EU. They suggest the EU can best be understood as multi-level governance which is multi-faceted with a multitude of actors or as enhanced transgovernmentalism.

On the other hand, it was obvious to others that the economic project, starting with the Treaty of Rome (1957) and developed by the Single European Act (1986), would develop a political superstructure sooner or later to protect its interests from internal and external threats.[34]

The failure to recognise that there is a European state is also because people are looking for a traditional national state at the EU level. This would involve the centralised direction and control of economic and social policies and practices, whereas in the EU implementation and variation (within broad norms) are largely left to implementation at national level. What may be true for the economic and social however does not hold for the political. For the political it is possible to trace a different historical path for the emergence of the *EU coercive state* which embraces internal and external security.

Ad hoc cooperation on terrorism (1976), policing and then immigration (1986) began under the Trevi arrangement and was formalised with the Maastricht Treaty (1993). The Amsterdam Treaty (1997) incorporated Schengen and its *acquis* from 1999 and the Nice Treaty (2000) heralded the beginnings of an independent military role in the world ('second pillar').

The current justice and home affairs (JHA) *acquis* – a body of laws and measures, some 'hard' law, some 'soft' law, some operational – is composed of the *acquis* of Trevi (1976-1993), Maastricht (1993-1999), Schengen (1980-2004) and Amsterdam (May 1999 and ongoing) *acquis* all rolled up into one. Some 800-plus measures and decisions form the JHA *acquis* which existing and applicant countries are obliged to implement in national law and put into effect.

What is significant about this great edifice of laws and practices is that it is a classic case of *a democracy built on sand*. All of the measures in the JHA *acquis* were adopted without national and European parliaments having a real say. The European Parliament was 'consulted' and its views routinely ignored. National parliaments have powers of 'scrutiny' (known as a 'scrutiny reservation') which is in effect 'consultation' and their views too are routinely overridden by governments.[35]

The policy programme for what is called in the EU 'justice and home affairs' (JHA, policing, immigration and asylum, and judicial cooperation) is set by the European Council (the 25 Prime Ministers).

The long-standing, embedded attitude of EU governments is that the 'real' negotiations take place in the meetings of officials and experts in the Council's working parties and high-level groups – not in parliaments or society at large.

The content of neither the 'Tampere' (1999-2004) or the 'Hague' (2004-2009) programmes were known in advance of their adoption by the European Council. The same goes for 'Action Plans', like the ones on terrorism and immigration adopted by the Council. These Programmes and Action Plans set the agenda for all the EU institutions and are adopted without any democratic debate.

It is possible to roughly divide the history of justice and home affairs into three periods:

1) the *ad hoc* Trevi era (1975-1993) which in its later years included meetings of Ministers and the creation of a Coordinators Group;

2) formalisation of the decision-making structure under the Maastricht Treaty (1993-1999). Creation of the Justice and Home Affairs Council of Ministers, high-level committees (eg: K4 Committee – named after an article in the Treaty) and working parties, and growth of the Council's General-Secretariat in Directorate General H (full-time officials and seconded national experts).

3) (1999 and ongoing) It was the Tampere Summit in 1999 that marked the beginning of the present era. Instead of individual proposals which often took years to get through (eg the Europol Convention) for the first time there was a comprehensive programme across the whole of justice and home affairs. Out is this programme came not just a raft of new measures but the growth of new bodies and agencies and operational powers for the General Secretariat in DG H (which is now the largest directorate-general in the Council). Some of the new bodies set up by the Council have no legal status and no mechanisms for accountability and scrutiny and are effectively self-regulating, for example, the Police Chiefs Task Force and the Joint Situation Centre (SitCen). What epitomises the emergence of the coercive (surveillance) state is the new Standing Committee on Internal Security (COSI). Although conceived as part of the EU Constitution it is one of the first to be rescued from the debris. In the two previous eras (Trevi and Maastricht) policing, immigration and judicial cooperation developed on independent tracks and tailored legal powers. Here for the first time the all-embracing concept of

'internal security' is employed – covering crime, terrorism, exchanging intelligence, 'public order management', 'illegal immigration and trafficking', 'integrated management systems for external borders' and crisis management (which could involve the military).[36]

The full-time officials in the Council's Directorate General H (Justice and Home Affairs) are supplemented by 'seconded national experts' (police, border guards, judges) who in addition to contributing to policy-making carry out missions to evaluate how the various elements of Action Plans (and the Schengen *acquis*) are being implemented.[37]

In the field of justice and home affairs the General Secretariat of the Council plays a quite different role to other policy areas. It plays the:

'role of a motor, legal drafter and initiative taker'[38].

It is usually the same official who goes to the various international fora that is drafting or is responsible for EU policy-making. In this field (internal security) there is a powerful, and quite small, nexus (coterie) of officials from national ministries, the Council's DG (JHA) and Commission representatives who are pivotal in determining and propagating policy options in the EU, G8 (and its working parties) and in discussions with the USA.

What also distinguishes the role of the Directorate-General for Justice and Home Affairs (within the General Secretariat of the Council) from other policy areas is that they are not just the 'motor' for policy-making but also increasingly undertake operational functions. For example, it is currently being proposed that the operational control of the new Schengen Information System (SIS II) is shared between the Council and the Commission. The idea that the EU governments, through the Council, should exercise operational control is outwith any democratic norm.[39] Moreover, in a number of areas like 'soft law' (Recommendations etc which are not subject to any parliamentary right of scrutiny) and operational matters the Council's Ministers and its officials are the executive, the legislature and the implementors.

The ability of parliaments and civil society to make their views known on policies and practices developed in the Council is severely limited. This is because the Council routinely refuses access to most documents when an issue is under discussion (or minutes which mentioned the discussions) before the final draft is agreed and published.[40] In other words, parliament and public are not allowed to know what differences, options and influences effect the final text. The Council is even more secretive when it comes to documents concerning third states, like the USA, which are routinely refused (or the relevant text censored) as this could undermine 'international relations'.[41]

The EU-US axis and its global influence
One of the enduring features of the 'war on terrorism' is the emergence of the 'EU-US axis'. There have always been regular meetings following on from the New Transatlantic Agenda (NTA, 1995) under which the EU-US Senior Officials Group and the EU-US Task Force met six-monthly. But after 11 September and the Bush letter to the EU of 16 October 2001 a new era of cooperation set in. Now, during each six-monthly EU Presidency there are at least twenty high-level meetings or video-conferences; US officials attend Council working parties and lobby the 'Troika' of EU Presidencies (current, past and future).[42]

This alliance in the 'war on terrorism' between the EU and the US is a major influence in G8 and its working parties – with the USA and UK in the lead.[43] This, in turn, links into the construction of global enforcement regimes.[44]

A classic case is the decision of the EU to introduce 'biometric' passports in December 2005.[45] It was argued that the EU needed to respond to international demands for 'biometric' travel documents in line with the adopted standard of the International Civil Aviation Organisation – a move emanating in G8 lead by the USA and the UK. The EU has used the ICAO recommendation, and the demands from the USA that any European going there must have a biometric passport to qualify for the US Visa Waiver Scheme, to introduce the wholesale surveillance of movement.

VI. The road ahead
The coercive European state has been constructed at the same time as liberal-democratic norms are ignored, abandoned, or declared redundant. New norms and morality are set by governments and the political class, and are honed and spun by officials. They result not from informed debate and political struggle, emerging over the years as a new consensus, rather they are handed down from on high.

The passing of principled values and morality are only too evident. The UN Declaration of Human Rights (1948) set out the aspirations of

31

liberal-democracy on economic, social and political rights. Today it reads like a radical document. The 1951 Geneva Convention on the rights of refugees and asylum-seekers has all but been written out of EU law. And now the protection given by the European Convention on Human Rights (ECHR) against people (who cannot be bought to trial for lack of evidence) being returned to countries where they would face 'torture or inhuman or degrading treatment or punishment' is being actively undermined by the UK (and is on the EU agenda too).

The slippage in language and intent, law and practices is frighteningly rapid. Terrorism is a problem and needs to be countered to prevent loss of life and injury. But what is terrorism? Charles Clarke, the former UK Home Secretary, told a parliamentary committee in October 2005 that it:

'cannot ever justify using violence to bring about change' (11.10.05)

When asked about Iraq he declined to answer.

If we look at history, is the 'use of violence to bring about change' to be applied to the (state) violence which led to the expansion and maintenance of the British Empire, or only to the mass civil disobedience and liberation movements which freed their peoples from colonialism?

Draconian measures have been put through before, but we have never seen such an assault on peoples' rights and democratic standards. What is happening has been characterised as 'sleepwalking into a surveillance society' (Richard Thomas, UK Information Commissioner) and the people of Europe are certainly doing that at the moment.

This is expressed as trading 'privacy for convenience', making life easier by having just one 'chipped' card for every transaction (eg: shopping, getting cash), entry (to work and flights) and verifying identity to get services (like education, health and welfare). Finger-printing, biometrics and databases to confirm identity make life easier and are directed at terrorists and serious organised criminals not at the great law-abiding majority. The notion that once in place and embedded in everyday life these same mechanisms will not be used for social control and the elimination of 'unacceptable' behaviour is dangerously naive.

But the danger goes much deeper than that, it is about the quality of the democracy we live in, the political culture, of which elections and parliaments are just a tiny part. At its most extreme 'representative democracy' simply means people vote every four or

Tony Bunyan

five years and then leave the politicians to get on with running their country (and the world). Governments are elected to get on with the job and the people 'should not be seen or heard' in-between elections. This was effectively the attitude of Bush and Blair on going to war in Iraq, ignoring the millions who took to the streets across the globe exercising the only power they had available.

To collude in the demise of democracy is to renounce any sense of responsibility for what is done in our name. Taken to its logical conclusion 'representative democracy' ends up legitimating (masking) the construction of an authoritarian era bringing self-regulated, unaccountable agencies and bodies exercising coercive powers. To be used first against 'suspected' terrorists (most are arrested, held, questioned and released) and unwanted 'illegal' immigrants who increasingly have no 'rights' – whether in detention centres across the EU or small boats in the Mediterranean.[46] And against protestors and those thought to hold 'extremist' and 'radical' opinions and dissenters and so on.[47]

The reaction of governments and states to terrorism go far beyond seeking to counter it. Rather the 'war on terrorism' is re-defining the political culture and re-defining democratic life beyond all recognition. The whole basis of a democracy is that when the basic rights and freedoms of the few are arbitrarily curtailed or removed so too are the rights and freedoms of us all.

The defence of rights and civil liberties in Europe, and globally, will determine whether 'democracy' has a future in any meaningful sense. There is an urgent need to unite people, whereever they are, into movements to 'resist and build' and to re-awaken the possibility of an alternative world based on humanity, compassion, equality, egalitarianism, diversity, tolerance and immutable rights and liberties for all.

Tony Bunyan is Director of Statewatch and editor of Statewatch Bulletin and Statewatch News Online.

Footnotes

1 In 2002 I wrote an analysis entitled 'The war on freedom and democracy', one year after 11 September. Nothing that has happened since leads me to change the views expressed there, but it is necessary to add and deepen an understanding of where we are going in Europe: see: http://www.statewatch.org/news/2002/sep/04freedom.htm

2 The seeds of this can be seen in the Conclusions of the Special EU Justice and Home Affairs Council meeting on 20 September 2001 and the Bush letter to the EU of 16 October:
http://www.statewatch.org/news/2001/nov/06uslet.htm Cooperation has included a Europol-US agreement, a Mutual Assistance agreement on extradition and judicial cooperation and the EU-US PNR (passenger name record) deal.

3 Sivanadan is Director of the Institute of Race Relations.

4 It should be remembered that Spain, Portugal and Greece lived under dictatorships for many years.

5 'Representative democracy', because of its lack of content and principled differences between the parties, is characterised by low voter turn-out, eg: USA around 50%, in UK 60% and the European election in 2004 just 45%. While in Egypt in 2005 only 22% voted for a number of reasons.

6 'Representative democracy' is not a theory but simply a description of the reality.

7 Values of course are not the same as basic principles, such as are enshrined in the Universal Declaration of Human Rights.

8 How this squares with the statement of Mr Blair, the UK Prime Minister, that the 'world has changed' and that some traditional rights and liberties have to be sacrificed is not clear.

9 In 2004 Afghanistan was declared 'safe' to send people back to – the EU decision however suggested that they should be given counselling as to the danger of unexploded ordinance (largely bombs dropped by US and UK planes).

10 One of the uses of the EU Galileo's space satellite programme will track boats and groups of people as they approach the borders.

11 An 'additional counter-terrorism initiative' currently being discussed is a feasibility study 'to register entries and exits of third country nationals' at Schengen area borders. This would check at borders on all third country nationals whether legally resident or entering with a visa. EU document: 11910/05: http://www.statewatch.org/news/2005/oct/eu-next-steps-05.pdf

12 This data is partly gathered by GCHQ and NSA independently and partly through the ECHELON system (run by them):
http://www.statewatch.org/news/2001/may/prechelon_en.pdf

13 'intelligence' is different to 'information'. 'Information' comprises hard facts, like, person's criminal record. 'Intelligence' on the other hand may be very good or highly doubtful depending on the source. 'Intelligence' is usually graded on a scale of 1 to 5 as to its accuracy.

14 Commission proposal: http://www.statewatch.org/news/2005/oct/com-dataprot-475.pdf

15 This is known as the 'pull' system, whereas a 'push' system is meant to be coming into effect whereby only that data needed is sent to the USA: see:

http://www.statewatch.org/news/2003/jul/09usdata.htm

16 http://www.statewatch.org/news/2005/oct/ba-usa.htm

17 There is a similar body in the EU whose status means that its reports carry a similar weight. The report of the Article 29 Working Party on Data Protection produces excellent reports, but as they are only 'consulted', these are routinely ignored.

18 It is not known who is on this list and it no doubt includes quite a number who would strongly dispute their inclusion.

19 Visa Information System (VIS), Final Report, April 2003, Trasys for the European Commission.

20 See: http://www.statewatch.org/news/2004/dec/07visas-residence-biometrics.htm

21 At this moment in time the EU is discussing a simpler matter, namely whether there should be exemptions for young children as they can be unreliable and change rapidly. Some member states suggested a minimum age of 12 years old but the majority, including the UK Presidency, wants 5 year of age – even if this means assigning finger-print experts to examine each set of prints at entry points where the children may have to be finger-printed again.

22 The European Parliament was only 'consulted' on this measure. Indeed it was blackmailed into giving its 'opinion' speedily. The Council of the European Union promised to extends the parliament's co-decision powers to immigration and asylum on 1 January 2005 instead of April 2005 – a move that gave the parliament co-decision powers, not consultation, over exactly measures like introducing biometric passports.

23 UK Presidency proposal: http://www.statewatch.org/news/2005/jul/07eu-id-bio-plan.htm

24 In the UK a National Health database is being created which will hold the personal medical records of everyone. It has been set up on the basis of 'opt-out' rather than 'opt-in' – it will happen unless an individual objects. The database will be accessible to over 500,000 medical staff. The EU started issuing a plastic EU Health Card (with no chip yet) in 2005 to replace the E111 form.

25 As distinct from filling out a form and sending with a picture in the post.

26 EU document no: 7416/05, 17.3.05.

27 EU Document no: 12511/05, 29.9.05.

28 This does not exclude the exchange of intelligence which was gathered by coercive means (eg: tapping or bugging) prior to the request for information. Moreover, there is a 'consensus' in the Council (as agreed at COREPER, the permanent Brussels-based representatives of the 25 governments, on 5 October 2005) that new coercive means could 'be obtained via mutual legal assistance.

29 EU doc no: 7416/05.

30 COM 221, 29.3.04 and see:
   http://www.statewatch.org/news/2004/jun/08eu-terrorism-and-crime.htm
31 Statewatch Scoreboard:
   http://www.statewatch.org/news/2004/mar/swscoreboard.pdf
32 HUMINT, human intelligence, is gathered by undercover agents or
   supplied by informants (willing and unwilling, paid and unpaid). Effective
   HUMINT takes years to put in place and even then is clearly less effective
   against an unstructured target with independent cells acting on their own
   initiative than a Cold War-style centrally organised state organisation.
33 'Group of Personalities:
   http://www.statewatch.org/news/2004/mar/swscoreboard.pdf and
   Commission first report:
   http://www.statewatch.org/news/2004/feb/security-research-com72.pdf and
   http://www.intelligenceonline.com/NETWORKS/FILES/468/468.asp?rub
   =networks
34 See, 'Towards an authoritarian European state', by Tony Bunyan, *Race and
   Class*, vol 32 no 3, January-March 1991.
35 On 1 January 2005 most of the decision-making powers on visas, asylum
   and immigration (in Title IV of the Treaty Establishing the European
   Community) moved to co-decision with the European Parliament.
36 EU document: 6626/05.
37 Although the Commission equivalent DG has an increasing right of
   initiative (eg in immigration and asylum) the final say is always with the
   Council – a proposal has to meet all the positions and objections of each
   national government.
38 *Council of the European Union*, Martin Westlake and David Galloway, p137.
39 For a number of years the Justice and Home Affairs Directorate General
   of the Council has had direct access to the Schengen Information
   System database in Strasbourg with access to individual records. When it
   comes to the EU the principle of the 'separation of powers' does not hold.
40 Under the 2001 Regulation on access to documents, 1049/2001, Article
   4.3.
41 op.cit, Article 4.4.
42 See for example, 'The exceptional and draconian become the norm',
   where US demands honed in G8 were then demanded of the EU:
   http://www.statewatch.org/news/2005/mar/exceptional-and-draconian.pdf
43 The other EU countries represented are France, Germany and Italy.
44 See the International Campaign Against Mass Surveillance: Report:
   http://www.statewatch.org/news/2005/apr/icams-report.pdf and website:
   http://www.i-cams.org/
45 The European Parliament was only 'consulted' on this measure. Indeed it
   was blackmailed into giving its 'opinion' speedily. The Council of the
   European Union promised to extend the parliament's co-decision powers

to immigration and asylum on 1 January 2005 instead of April 2005 – a move that gave the parliament co-decision powers, not consultation, over exactly measures like introducing biometric passports.

46 A measure now going through the EU institutions – on which there is a consensus between Council, Commission and European Parliament – on the procedural rights for all suspects, like right to bail, a lawyer, access to family, translators etc, excludes giving these rights to terrorist 'suspects'. How many 'suspects' have been arrested and held for questioning across Europe since 2001 but later released for lack of evidence?

47 Six civil liberties campaigners for the UK NO2ID (identity cards) went to Newcastle in two cars in September to protest outside the Informal Meeting of EU Justice and Home Affairs Ministers. They got nowhere near the meeting because they were arrested by police 'on suspicion of conspiracy to commit criminal damage and are currently in custody'. This small, peaceful protest was arbitrarily stopped when it presented no threat to anyone. BBC News, 8.9.05.

5

Lex Vigilatoria –
Towards a control system without a state?

Thomas Mathiesen

In 1997, Gunther Teubner edited *Global Law without a State*.[1] Among the interesting contributions to the volume is Gunther Teubner's own introductory piece 'Global Bukowina: Legal Pluralism in the World Society' (pp. 3-28). Teubner's main concern is the development of *lex mercatoria*, the transnational law of economic transactions, mostly transnational contract law, which he views as 'the most successful example of global law without a state' (p. 3). Global law, according to Teubner, has some characteristics which are 'significantly different from our experience of the law of the nation-state' (p. 7):

– The boundaries of global law are not formed by maintaining a core territory and possibly expanding from this, but rather by invisible social networks, invisible professional communities, invisible markets which transcend territorial boundaries.

– General legislative bodies are less important – global law is produced in self-organised processes of what Teubner calls 'structural coupling' of law with ongoing globalised processes which are very specialised and technical.

– Global law exists in a diffuse but close dependence, not on the institutional arrangements of nation-states (such as parliaments) but, on their respective specialised social fields – in the case of *lex mercatoria*, the whole development of the expanding and global economy.

– For nation-building in the past unity of law was a main political asset. A world wide unity of law would become a threat to legal culture. It would be important to make sure that a sufficient variety of legal sources exists in a globally unified law.

In my own words, *lex mercatoria* is a: Transnational economic law developed, not by committees and councils and established by ministries in nation-states and subsequently given sanction by parliaments but, through the work of the large and expanding professional lawyers' firms, the jet-set lawyers operating on the transnational level, tying vast capital interests together in complex agreements furthering capital interests. As *lex mercatoria* develops, it is not given subsequent primary sanction by national parliaments but is self-referential and self-validating, finding suitable 'landing points' in quasi-legislative institutions (Teubner p. 17) such as international chambers of commerce, international law associations, and all sorts of international business associations. It develops as a system of customary law in a diffuse zone around the valid formal law of nation-states, not inside valid formal law but not too far outside it. Eventually it becomes regarded as (equivalent to) valid formal law, or at least valid legal interpretation. It develops continuously, one step building on the other, in the end validating a law or a set of legal interpretations far from the law of the nation-states.

The increasingly independent and self-sufficient development of such a legal arrangement is the crux of the matter. Ideally global *lex mercatoria* develops of its own accord, based on its own internal sociological logic. There is a great debate going on concerning the independence of global *lex mercatoria* – Teubner calls it a thirty years' war. I will not enter that war here, but simply ask the question: Do we, in recent developments in the late twentieth and early twenty-first centuries, see signs of a developing, independent global control system as a kind of frightening *lex vigilatoria* of surveillance and subsequent political control? Global control without a state?

The question is complex. There are certainly ties between nation-states in the EU and say Schengen, the SIRENE exchange, Eurodac, communication control through retention and tapping of telecommunications traffic data, the spy system Echelon and so on. For one thing, some of these systems are established on the national level first. The recent British proposal to the EU (in July 2005, after the terrorist onslaught in London on July 7th) to make the retention of a wide range of telecommunications traffic data for a year, or more, mandatory in all member states is an example (though this may be viewed as a strategic way of getting a common system off the ground – note the related proposal from the EU Commission in October 2005). Secondly, some of the systems are established through various joint national efforts. Some of the joint national efforts are complex (meetings and memos over ten years concerning communications control; the lengthy negotiations over Schengen), some of them are simpler (framework decisions, involving agreements of ministers from the nation-states), some of them are very simple (quick common positions cleared by governments). Thirdly, agreements such as partnerships in Schengen, Europol and Eurodac have to be sanctioned by national parliaments.

But, at the same time, there are signs suggesting that systems such as the ones I have mentioned are becoming increasingly untied or 'decoupled' (to use Teubner's term) from the nation-states. For one thing, the parliamentary nation-state sanctioning of arrangements such as Schengen, Europol and Eurodac to a considerable extent takes place without in depth debates in public space, and, significantly, without parties and members of parliaments really knowing to any degree of detail the systems they are sanctioning. Parties and members must necessarily trust the work being done by various sub-committees and officials, and so on, deep inside the EU structure, over and above agencies of the nation-states. There is neither time nor motive for anything else. An example is the scrutiny of the various *acquis*, enormous heaps of documents drastically reducing transparency for an ordinary parliament member (or even a researcher).

Furthermore, once the various systems are up and running they interlock, through informal agreements and arrangements, and so rapidly expand their practices (a kind of customary law, again in the diffuse zone around valid formal law). In other words, the systems are increasingly integrated '*horizontally*'. There are numerous examples of this.[2] There seems to be an important relationship between the '*horizontal*' integration, or interlocking, aspects of the various systems and the '*vertical*' weakening of ties, or de-coupling aspects, to nation-state agencies: The more integrated or interlocked the systems become ('horizontal' integration), the more independent of, or de-coupled, from national state institutions they will be ('vertical' weakening of ties) when the agendas for future developments and operations are set. Integration and interlocking links the systems together in functional terms. Given moves are, therefore, simply regarded as 'necessary' or imperative, irrespective of the thinking which might be valid on the nation-state level. Interlocking at the system level also makes particular developments seem imperative from the point of view of the nation-state level. For example, the 'package' consisting of the Schengen Information System, Europol and Eurodac, in which all three systems are increasingly intertwined in terms of cooperation and goals, has made it increasingly 'obvious' and 'necessary' for Norway to participate in all three of them, if not without debate, then at least with a minimum of debate. The question of Norwegian participation in the first of these, the Schengen Information System, created some critical debate. Norwegian participation in Europol and Eurodac hardly reached the newspapers or television at all.

The horizontal integration of the systems expands by internal sociological forces far from the control of nation-state institutions. Eventually the horizontal interlockings and the vertical de-couplings are taken as *givens* simply to be reckoned with. System functionaries – and all together there are thousands of them – take pride and find legitimacy in such developments. They become part and parcel of their systems, they find colleagues, and even emotional attachments in their systems, they define their particular system as something they should foster, feeling great satisfaction when they manage to make the system function still better. These are entirely commonplace processes; this is how we all become more or less enveloped by the systems we are working in.[3] A small example: In a discussion with Norwegian Schengen personnel some years ago, I ventured the guess that their doings were not all that rational after all – they probably took great pride and satisfaction in the computerised technical and complex activities they were involved in and were continuously developing. The response was instant – fumbling with papers, some blushing, some openly agreeing.

To be sure, the various horizontally interlocking systems have their national 'landing points', although, much like *lex mercatoria,* not through strong vertical ties to responsible and authoritative parliamentary settings but, in quasi-legislative institutions – in this case especially branches of the law enforcement agencies with their strongly vested interests.

Conclusion

A cautious conclusion for the time being: I would say that there is a development towards increasingly diluted ties to the institutions of the nation-states. While not global law fully without a state, a dilution of connections with the formal institutions of the nation-state is taking place. Most significantly, the institution of parliamentary sanction has become, at least in many European states, a perfunctory exercise with a silent public as a context.

But perhaps a 'state' is re-entering the scene on a different level? At least as far as the European control systems are concerned, the importance of the institutions of the European Union is enhanced as the nation-state institutions fade.[4] Any state, also a European State, requires certain institutions: one of them is policing (but not necessarily of the kind we are witnessing today).

However, the European control systems, though largely emanating from the EU, also have tentacles far beyond the EU, interlocking horizontally with various systems of control in the US and other parts of the Western world. The EU-FBI attempts, pointed out so clearly by Statewatch, to develop transnational communication control over the last ten years is a case in point.

Are we, then, facing once again a developing, unfinished, expanding global control, if not without a state so at least with increasingly diluted ties to state institutions? Is a *lex vigilatoria*, if not developing entirely of its own accord, at least with strong internal sociological forces leading the development and control measures, increasingly out of state control?

If so, we need to understand these sociological forces better if we are to oppose and contain them. A penetrating and critical research project exactly on this, for example under the auspices of Statewatch, would be in order. Such a project could develop into a counter-force. From a critical point of view, it is vital to stem this tide before it is too late.

Thomas Mathiesen is Professor of Sociology of Law, Oslo.

Footnotes

1 Aldershot: Dartmouth Publishing.

2 See my 'The Rise of the Surveillant State in Times of Globalization'. In Colin Sumner (ed.), *The Blackwell Companion to Criminology*, Oxford: Blackwell Publishing 2004, pp. 437-451.

3 See my *Silently Silenced. Essays on the Creation of Acquiescence in Modern Society.* Winchester: Waterside Press 2004.

4 It is possible that the European state may be taking a different form to that at the national level. While it is not evident in the 'first pillar' (economic and social affairs) it is arguable that since the Tampere Summit (October 1999) the 'third pillar' (policing, immigration, judicial cooperation, internal security) is adopting EU-wide 'state' functions and roles. The same may be said of the 'second pillar' (military and foreign policy) since the Nice Treaty (2000). If this is so then maybe we are seeing the construction of a 'coercive' EU state.

6

Checks and balances in the EU polity

Deirdre Curtin

'Is the Council aware of any website maintained by a European public authority which is better designed to frustrate the ability of citizens to access information than that of the Council of Ministers?'[1]

From Market to State?

The days of the European Union being, what some termed, a 'market without a state'[2] or a 'stateless market'[3] are long past. Back in the days before the Treaty of Maastricht and the leap to more overtly *political* integration, the European integration process could indeed be conceived as, in its core, about the construction and consolidation among the constituent Member States of a free market (an 'internal market'). It was a fairly win-win scenario with markets being opened up for the benefit of traders and consumers by a combination of judicial activism, legislative harmonization, mutual recognition of (product) standards and technical standardization. There were of course inroads made into national sovereignty and national laws had to be disapplied (on occasion) but the inroads were in the field of economic law (and later some 'flanking' issues such as the environment and consumer protection). Of course all of this could be considered necessary foundations in order to achieve the long-term goal of a more political federation. This is certainly what the federalists and neo-functionalists believed; the integration process was moving forward step-by-step towards – some day – a more overtly *political* union. In the meantime what was termed (and largely accepted by the so-called passive consensus that existed among the national political classes) 'integration by stealth' could progress, little by little, with the bureaucrats (and at times the judges) firmly in the driving seat.

The Treaty of Maastricht can, in many ways, be considered the very explicit crossroads, the moment that the EU's politicians signalled both internally and externally that it would henceforth also be integrating areas such as justice and home affairs within the institutional framework originally conceived for purely market integration. Gradually as the decade of the inter-governmental conferences advanced (in the 1990s) changes were made in the legal frameworks and the legal instruments in a manner that consolidated ambitions in this – qualitatively different – area. The scenario shifted at the same time from a relatively optimistic win-win one to a more troubled scenario with very clear winners and *losers*.

The winners in this incremental process have this time not been individual citizens or companies but rather their statal executive counter-parts in the constituent Member States themselves and, at times, at the central EU level too. Thus we have seen the powers increased and the role strengthened of sub-state authorities such as the police, customs and enforcement authorities more generally. Moreover, we have seen the establishment of more operational executive type bodies at EU level itself (such as Europol and the External Borders Agency) as well as extensive databases being administered by EU institutions (for example in the case of Schengen Information System II it is proposed that it will be managed jointly by the Commission and the Council General Secretariat[4], in explicit recognition it seems of the split nature of the EU executive).The losers, sadly, have tended to be the individual citizens and non-citizens who have seen their rights and interests adversely affected by the changes that have been made and their civil liberties often challenged and eroded.

For more than a decade then, the European Union has, as a matter of empirical and normative fact, been more than a market with or without a state. That 'more' has ever so incrementally grown to the point that one can, in my opinion, consider the EU to have inched closer towards what it means to be a 'state' in today's world. This is not to say that the EU can be compared in all respects to a state – this is clearly not the case. But what it has done is in the past decade or more is two-fold. On the one hand, it has, at the centralized EU level, acquired certain specific trappings of 'states'. On the other hand, it has taken the logic and the instruments of the internal market and sought to transplant them beyond the market and the world of companies, traders and consumers to the very core of state power, criminal law, the powers of enforcement authorities and intelligence actors etc. In the manner of its so doing the hypothesis might well be that it has shifted the paradigm of the EU: from market to – dare one put it in such politically incorrect terms these days – to (non-) state.

Refining the paradigm: enter trans-governmental networks
At the same time, even as a hypothesis, this is too strong in terms of the absolute images it sketches. The EU is clearly not on the road to

becoming a (federal-type) state as such, at least not in the short or medium term. The Member States have not overtly delegated their powers say in the field of criminal law or of internal security to the EU so that the EU can now assert itself as such in their place in these fields. The EU is as dependent as ever on the judges, the courts, the administrations, the police, the intelligence actors, etc, of the individual Member States. It has not replaced these as such at the central level.

The point is rather to frame what is happening in terms of the type of polity that is emerging as a matter of empirical and normative practice. The EU is, as a matter of legal and institutional practice, increasingly empowering (sub-) state actors and national authorities in various fields to integrate their practices. What is happening is, however, not so easy to see and to evaluate as the process of integration by stealth shifts even further underground as a result of the failure to ratify the Constitutional Treaty. It entails the imposition at the EU level of the institutional parameters and requirements mandating what can be termed advanced 'trans-governmentalism' among various core state actors. A good example of this phenomenon is the recent draft Framework Decision on simplifying the exchange of information and intelligence between law enforcement authorities of the Member States of the European Union (not yet available in PDF file on the Council's Register of its Documents[5]). The basic idea is the free movement of information held in databases that are owned by the competent enforcement authorities or information that is 'available' to them (including information available in other State and private databases). The principle of availability requires that authorities in one Member State exchange all information available with other authorities in other Member States in the same way and under the same conditions as they do within their own jurisdiction. The definition of 'competent enforcement authorities' in the current draft is:

> *'a national police, customs or other authorities, that is authorized by national law to detect, prevent or investigate offences or criminal activities and to exercise authority and take coercive measures in the context of such activities'*

This clearly seems to include within its scope security and intelligence agencies. The Framework Decision does not prohibit use of information supplied in this fashion as evidence in criminal proceedings nor does it restrict it by setting either procedural or substantive conditions. This is a complex subject that clearly raises important issues with implications for civil liberties of affected individuals. Apart from these substantive issues it highlights the problematic manner in which the Council reaches its decisions in such highly sensitive areas: very largely behind closed doors.

Checks and balances?

In the aftermath of the 'Non' and the 'Nee', and the feelings of consternation that prevail, there does seem to be some growing sense that this situation opens a window of opportunity to discuss why the gulf between the continuing processes of 'integration by stealth' meets with incomprehension and outright rejection by (many) of the citizens. Moreover, leaving the C word to one side, with all its state-like baggage, what can be done to ensure that it is not just business as usual but in the absence of a Constitution? In other words, what can be done now in the absence of any grand project of reform to ensure that, nonetheless, the integration process that proceeds at the level of 'low politics' in Brussels and Member State capitals can operate within a more accountable framework, with some more measures checking and balancing the on-going exercise of power?

In my view a lot more can be achieved on the subject of freedom of information in the EU especially at this critical juncture of a constitutional impasse. There is no reason why the Council cannot, in line with a recent recommendation from the European Ombudsman, decide quite simply itself (and revise in this sense its own internal Rules of Procedure) to henceforth meet *in public* whenever it is acting in its legislative capacity. This seems to be a very basic first step that can be followed by some serious discussion and debate on the scope of the Council's executive (and even) operational tasks and to see to what extent such processes and the underlying information and documents can also be opened up or at the very least be made available publicly.

In the context of the European Union it seems particularly appropriate to focus on the issue of the *public* nature of decision-making given its bad reputation for secretive decision-taking behind closed doors. One aspect deserving to be highlighted is the fact that a very crucial part of the executive and legislative structures in the EU, namely those involving the Council of Ministers and the increasingly important European Council are often set apart from debates on increasing public deliberation in various processes of the EU. In other words not only is the Council not engaging with non-bureaucratic actors in a deliberative fashion prior to decision-taking, there are entire largely non-public conclaves nestling within its institutional structures. This is true not only in relation to the newer policy areas of foreign and security policy and justice and home affairs, although these policy areas have certainly helped to bring the problem more to the fore. There is a mismatch between the rhetoric and practice on transparency and public access to its documents and the Council's secretive structures and rule-making processes, especially in the more executive sphere of activity.

At the launch of the European Civil Liberties Network by Statewatch it seems to be very timely to raise as they have done the need for an EU Freedom of Information instrument that would impose tailored obligations on both the EU level (all institutions, actors and networks) on the one hand and on the Member State level (all authorities and actors implementing or fulfilling Union obligations). Surely the time has come to re-launch the debate in a holistic fashion by focusing on the various sites within the institutional configuration of the EU where executive tasks are carried out with the ambition of formulating and applying horizontal principles on publicity, debate and participation?

Deirdre Curtin is Professor of European and International Governance, Utrecht School of Governance, Utrecht, Netherlands.

Footnotes

1 Parliamentary Question by Chris Davies, MEP to the Council, 14 July 2005. The question is slightly disingenuous given the fact that both the European Parliament itself and the Council have far from perfect web-sites themselves.

2 C.Joerges, 'The Market Without the State? The "Economic Constitution" of the European Community and the Rebirth of Regulatory Politics', European Integration Online Papers, vol 1, no.19, http://eiop.or.at

3 P.Kapteyn, *The Stateless Market. The European dilemma of integration and civilisation.* (Routledge, 1996)

4 SIS II: Resource management and increased support to improve national co-ordination, Council Document 12721/05, 5 October 2005.

5 But see, Statewatch, www.statewatch.org

7

There is no 'balance' between security and civil liberties – just less of each

Ben Hayes

In a speech in September 2005 to the European Parliament, then UK
Home Secretary Charles Clarke made the following statements:

> 'We now possess many hard-fought rights such as the right to privacy, the right to
> property, the right to free speech and the right to life. Those rights are actively
> threatened by criminals and terrorists ...
>
> [I]t is necessary to look very carefully at the way in which the jurisprudence
> around application of the European Convention on Human Rights is developing.
> This Convention, established over 50 years ago in a quite different international
> climate has led to great advances in human rights across the continent.
>
> [But] the view of my Government is that this balance is not right for the
> circumstances which we now face – circumstances very different from those faced by
> the founding fathers of the European Convention on Human Rights – and that it
> needs to be closely examined in that context'.[1]

Clarke's view is by no means a new one. At every opportunity since the
onset of the 'war on terror' governments have been quick to stress the
need to 'rethink' the balance between civil liberties and security. Many
academics too are fond of this idea, promoting the hypothesis that it
is now somehow necessary to 'trade' a few of our civil liberties for 'a
bit more security'.

This is a myth that now masks a sustained attack on civil liberties by
a state that has been growing more coercive and less democratic for
decades.[2] It is true that some individual rights are not absolute and
must be balanced against those of others, but how can there be a
'trade-off' between (collective) liberties and (collective) security if both
are in decline? The participation of UK forces in Iraq and Afghanistan
and, increasingly, the conduct of the domestic 'war on terror' have
made us less secure, while a host of parliamentary acts have made us
less free. Less liberty, less security – just a more powerful state
apparatus, and a more powerful executive.

This is what lies behind Charles Clarke's contempt for the
European Convention on Human Rights, and why his speech earned
such an outraged response from Rene van der Linden, president of
the Council of Europe parliamentary assembly, who attempted to

remind those of us in Britain that the European Convention was drawn-up in the wake of the atrocities of World War II and German fascism as a set of minimum standards for the treatment of human beings by democratic states.[3] Times have changed only in that the powers the government now wants to combat terrorism (and other crimes) treat suspects and defendants below these 50-year-old norms. It is not criminals or terrorists that threaten human rights or give them their significance, but the actual and potential breach of those rights by the state. It is for this reason that Clarke praises only rights that rarely or never get in the way of counter-terrorism policy.[4] And it is for this reason that the circumstances facing Clarke's 'founding fathers' are no different to those of today.

Overcompensating: UK counter-terrorism law before September 11
In 2000, two acts of parliament gave the UK police comprehensive powers to prevent, investigate and prosecute acts of terrorism and place suspects under sustained surveillance: the Terrorism Act and Regulation of Investigatory Powers Act (RIPA). The Terrorism Act 2000 made permanent decades of 'emergency' terrorism law in spite of the ceasefire in Northern Ireland and has a number of features that make it among the most developed counterterrorism legislation in the world: it extends powers of stop and search of persons and vehicles without grounds for suspicion; it allows police to interrogate suspects for up to seven (extended in 2004 to 14) days without charge; it allows premises to be searched without a warrant; it allows the designation of 'emergency' areas granting 'special' powers to the police (London has been in a permanent state of emergency as far as the Act is concerned since September 11); it allows the Home Secretary to proscribe foreign terrorist groups, criminalising membership and support; it allows the prosecution in the UK courts of individuals accused of supporting or participating in acts of terrorism anywhere in the world; and it introduced a host of criminal offences that carry a maximum of 10-14 years in prison, including the possession of any article or document that might be used for terrorism, giving or receiving or terrorist training and supporting a terrorist group.

To this can be added the provisions in the Act which empower the Home secretary – not the courts – to authorise the surveillance of all communications of an individual or whole group; allows all forms of covert surveillance without a warrant; and creates a criminal offence of failing to provide the police with an encryption key.[5] People often talk about the US Patriot Act legitimising intrusive state surveillance but it does not even come close to the Regulation of Investigatory Powers Act.

So before September 11 the police had all powers required to investigate suspected terrorists, place them under intensive surveillance, and arrest and prosecute them as soon as any evidence to suggest any involvement whatsoever in terrorism came to light. This is not to say that efforts to improve security were not needed, just that these efforts should have centred on resource issues such as manpower, equipment and competence rather than sweeping new powers for the police.

Perverting the cause of justice: UK counter-terrorism law since September 11
What has happened since 11 September 2001 mirrors precisely the discredited course of action taken by successive British governments in Northern Ireland. First, we see the construction of a separate criminal justice system to deal with 'suspected' terrorists. Second, measures introduced in the name of 'counter-terrorism' or 'security' are used for ordinary policing and public order situations.[6]

Internment was re-introduced under the Antiterrorism, Crime and Security Act 2001 and the notoriously unlawful derogation from the right to a fair trial under the European Convention on Human Rights. On 15 December 2001, ten individuals were seized from their homes and taken straight to Belmarsh and Woodhill high security prisons. No one was told of their arrest and their families had no idea what had happened to them or where they had gone. By chance a number of them arrived on a landing in Belmarsh Prison where a remand prisoner who had a phone card was able to phone his solicitor and inform her that a number of people had arrived, they were not being allowed to make phone calls, and they needed a lawyer urgently. Belmarsh refused visits until after Christmas.

In total 17 Muslim men were detained under ATCSA for up to three years without charge. Just prior to their release a medical report found 'serious damage to the health of all the detainees';[7] three were moved to Broadmoor (a high-security hospital) as a result of their detention. When the Act was declared unlawful by the House of Lords, parliament simply replaced internment with house arrest, twenty-four hour surveillance and control orders. Eleven of the ATCSA internees received control orders within days of the legislation being rushed through parliament.

The control orders system is only slightly less draconian than its unlawful predecessor. It is based, crucially, on the principle of secret evidence from the security services. This evidence has been found to be based on dubious testimony from informants (including terrorist 'supergrasses'), 'evidence' obtained through torture or inhumane treatment (which is notoriously unreliable as well as unlawful), and material obtained through unregulated surveillance – all of which, for obvious reasons, the security services do not want tested in open court.

As Gareth Peirce, who represented some of the men interned under ATSCA, explains:

> 'all of this construct is created to avoid our constitutional protections of fair, public and open trial, by a jury of your peers, in which the most important aspect of all is that your accuser tells you at the earliest possible moment what the accusation against you is, so that you have the opportunity of replying. None of this construct can be improved or affected by amendments since the very purpose of the new legislation is to avoid these central obligations. Once the individual is branded [a terrorist], any information to justify the branding is considered behind closed doors.'[8]

Covert investigations, secret evidence, executive decisions
While there can be no excuse, ever, for the acceptance of evidence obtained through torture,[9] the Court of Appeal ruled astonishingly that as long as the UK was not complicit in the torture (i.e. it happened abroad) it can be used against terrorist suspects in Britain. In a world of extraordinary renditions and the well-documented 'outsourcing' of torture[10] this judgment was an affront to human rights. Again, Gareth Peirce explains why:

> 'We should not be deceived. What is happening in Guantanamo; what is happening in the secret hearings with foreign nationals already taking place in this country; and what is proposed for the future, is in the nature of an ongoing experiment. This is the pooling of access to internationally condemned methods of investigation. Since their utilisation will be covert, the overt experiment is into how willing the public of this country and those concerned in the passage of legislation are to allow basic safeguards to be jettisoned without protest.'[11]

The attempt to introduce detention without charge for three months for 'suspected terrorists' certainly felt like an instalment of that experiment.

Executive powers, generally reserved to the Home Office, have developed in tandem with those for the police; both come at the expense of the criminal justice system. The Terrorism Act 2000 allows the Home Secretary to ban foreign 'terrorist' organisations but offers proscribed organisations only a limited form of appeal to a special tribunal (secret hearings, secret evidence, special procedures etc). It is clear that the proscription of a number of the groups on the list (currently 25 though 15 more are pending at the time of writing)[12] is not about disrupting their activities – since few are active in, or pose any threat to the UK – but about appeasing foreign governments by prosecuting their political opponents in Britain. This often means that people who have been exiled from their own countries for their political activities and then recognised as refugees in the UK for this reason are now again being prosecuted for their political beliefs. It does not matter if these people were exercising what most people see as a legitimate right to resist occupation and tyranny because Charles Clarke cannot think of any situation in the world where 'violence would be justified to bring about change'.[13] So the illegal invasion of Iraq by the US and UK was justified, but the Palestinian Intifada, for example, is not. This position is not just hypocritical: the criminalisation of liberation struggles brings with it the criminalisation of solidarity.[14]

Unacceptable behaviour
Under the latest raft proposals it will also be for the Home Secretary to decide which kinds of 'terrorist' acts it will be illegal to 'glorify' in accordance with the planned new offence of 'glorifying terrorism' – a blatant clampdown on one of Charles Clarke's 'hard fought' rights. And it is the Home Office that has drawn-up a list of 'unacceptable behaviours' which will be grounds for deporting individuals who the Home Secretary believes have behaved unacceptably. This list could hardly have been cast any wider:

> *'writing, producing, publishing or distributing material; public speaking including preaching; running a website; or using a position of responsibility such as teacher, community or youth leader to express views which: foment, justify or glorify terrorist violence in furtherance of particular beliefs; seek to provoke others to terrorist acts; foment other serious criminal activity or seek to provoke others to serious criminal acts; or foster hatred which might lead to inter-community violence in the UK'.*[15]

Add to this the Nationality, Immigration and Asylum Act 2002, which gave the Home Secretary the power to strip UK citizenship from any individual with dual nationality on national security grounds (the so-called 'Abu Hamza law', a law that spectacularly failed to strip Mr. Abu Hamza of his British citizenship).

Tony Blair and Charles Clarke are adamant that neither the courts nor the European Convention on Human Rights will stand in the way of their desire to deport Muslims that they believe are guilty of 'fermenting hate' (let us be clear that this is who the law is aimed at). Never mind that these people have entered and resided in the UK lawfully, have not been convicted of any criminal offence, or face likely torture upon their return to the regimes they have fled. No-one can disagree with the principle that people who are guilty of inciting or planning acts of terrorism in this country should be expelled, but it should always be for the courts and not the executive to decide who is guilty of what.

None of the men seized in the well publicised raids on 'terrorists' who face deportation at the Home Secretary's behest appear to have been convicted of involvement in terrorism or any related offence by the UK courts – non-nationals imprisoned for most criminal offences are routinely deported anyway. What has happened with the recent 'security deportations' is that first, the police rounded-up the 'usual suspects' – the mainly Algerian men who had long been interned in Belmarsh and then placed under house arrest with control orders. Back in prison pending deportation one of the men attempted to hang himself. These arrests (and the suicide attempt) in the wake of the July 7 bombings, reflect a desperate desire on the part of the government to be seen to be doing something, regardless of whether it is the right thing. This does not inspire confidence in the handling of the terrorist threat.

But it is the 'terrorist' arrests pending deportation that really incense. In April 2005 more Algerian men were acquitted of any involvement in the 'ricin plot' in near farce because of the astonishing lack of evidence presented by the prosecution – it was a far cry from when Tony Blair and Colin Powell cited the 'foiled plot' at the UN Security Council as part of their justification for invading Iraq. On 15 September 2005 the acquitted, who are recognised as political refugees by the UK, were re-arrested pending deportation to Algeria. This prompted three of the jurors in their trial to take the brave and unprecedented step of repeating their unequivocal view that the men were completely innocent and condemning the arrests in a BBC documentary.[16] 'Police state' said one, using words that should be used lightly by anyone – but what else can be said about the seizure of men acquitted by the courts only to be incarcerated and banished to face likely torture on the say-so of a government minister?

Special powers, ordinary policing
The host of 'special powers' to combat 'terrorism' or increase 'security' include a number of measures that are applied to or geared entirely toward 'normal policing'. A situation predicted by civil liberties groups is the routine use of terrorism legislation to combat demonstrations and to stop-and-search protestors.[17] The Serious Organised Crime and Police Act 2005 can also be mentioned here, including as it does the now infamous clause banning demonstrations within a kilometre of London's parliament square (the 'Brian Haw law', not the first time that parliament has passed a law aimed at a single individual that threatens the rights of many).[18]

New Labour's latest take on 'unacceptable behaviour' saw an 82 year-old delegate being dragged from the 2005 party conference for shouting 'nonsense' during Jack Straw's speech on Iraq (not the first time a Labour heckler has been swiftly dealt with by burly security guards). Things went from bad to worse for the government as it emerged that not only was this expellee a life-long party member who had come to Britain after escaping the Nazi regime, but that he had subsequently been questioned by the police under Section 44 of the Terrorism Act.

Terrorism has also been used to justify sweeping changes to the extradition system. In 2003 the UK government signed, in secret, with no prior consultation of parliament, a new extradition treaty with the United States. This treaty has the effect of removing the obligation on the US to provide *prima facie* evidence when seeking the extradition of people from the UK (including UK nationals), not just for terrorism but for any offence publishable by a year a more in prison. But while the US need now only supply a statement of the facts to extradite someone from the UK, the UK must still supply *prima facie* evidence when seeking to extradite someone from the US – it is entirely and inexplicably one-sided.[19] The UK implemented the treaty on the back of the European Arrest Warrant implementing legislation in 2004; the US has not even bothered to ratify it (so the 1972 rules still apply where Britain wants to extradite). The US has since filed a number of blatantly unjust extradition requests to the UK in accordance with new treaty.

In 2004 the Civil Contingencies Act was passed, giving the government of the day the power to impose what pretty much amounts to martial law during 'emergencies'. Again, these are not limited to terrorist attack, war or natural disaster but defined much more broadly as any 'event or situation' which threatens 'serious damage' to 'human welfare', 'the environment' or 'security'. This Act takes powers devised during the Second World War to a new level. During future emergencies the government will be able to pass law without consulting parliament.

The Inquiries Act 2005 is not unrelated to the 'war on terrorism'. This Act does away with many of the key features of 'public inquiries' as we once knew them. Parliament can no longer authorise a public enquiry, only the government of the day. And it is for that government to decide the terms of reference, appoint the judge, decide whether proceedings and reports should be public, and terminate the 'public enquiry' at any stage. As things stand it is safe to say we will not see the likes of even the limited Hutton inquiry again, though this – based in no small part on Blair's ignominy for that inquiry – was the purpose of the Act.

Finally, the ID cards bill will bequeath the police a dedicated, updatable population register and fingerprint database and encourage yet more stop checks on 'suspect communities'. This is so, despite both Clarke and Blair freely admitting that 'all the surveillance in the world' could not have prevented the London bombings. The principle that democratic societies only fingerprint criminals has endured the world over for more than a century. It has now been replaced at a stroke by the wisdom that we should fingerprint entire populations, proving that we really are all suspects now.

Laws of diminishing return

It is fundamental that the current government be held to account over both the war in Iraq and the domestic 'war on terror'. The former is a 'recruiting sergeant' for al-Qaeda and a breeding ground for future terrorism and the latter is detrimental to rights and liberties. If 'all the surveillance in the world' cannot prevent four young British men blowing themselves up in rush-hour London crowds, what can? What are the lessons that should really be drawn from this tragedy?

The only thing we can be sure of is that '7/7' was a political act inspired directly by the war in Iraq.[20] This first lesson is alas one that the government can only deny – that UK foreign policy is capable of provoking this kind of reaction. Quite how the four were 'radicalised' and how they acquired the expertise to carry out the attack is still unknown, but the failure to yet find any 'mastermind' behind the conspiracy is irrelevant. The age-old second lesson is a cliché: it's the quiet ones you have to watch. And while the government admits that you can't possibly watch everyone, this is the course it is pursuing (never mind that if you are watching everyone, you're really watching no-one). The only role here is for families and communities, none of whom want their children to grow-up to be suicide bombers.

While the government professes to be reaching out to the Muslim and Asian communities in Britain, it is instead embarking on a 'war on Islamic extremism'. This new front in the 'war on terror' is based on the premise that the four young British men who carried out the bombings were 'brainwashed' by predatory 'extremists' (a view that is understandably shared by their families). The idea of a terrorist mastermind, preferably an 'al-Qaeda lieutenant', who recruited these men at a 'radical Mosque' and then 'brainwashed' them is inherently more palatable than the idea that these young British men were driven to do this by their sense of injustice (and that others might be so again). But it is a pretext for the claim that London was attacked not because it has troops 'defending an emerging democracy in Iraq', but because Britain has for too long been allowed to become a haven for 'Islamic extremism'. 'The hate that surges through the Islamic world surges through London' is how George Bush's former speechwriter put. Tony Blair was only slightly more subtle, blaming the bombings on 'their barbaric ideas':

> *'They demand the elimination of Israel; the withdrawal of all Westerners from Muslim countries, irrespective of the wishes of people and government; the establishment of effectively Taleban states and Sharia law in the Arab world en route to one caliphate of all Muslim nations.'*[21]

This inflammatory distortion of why Britain was bombed – by its own – is what underpins the new 'war on Islamic extremism'. It is the basis for banning non-violent, political organisations like Hizb-ut-Tahrir. It is the basis for rounding-up the 'preachers of hate' and, in doing so, making martyrs of the loudmouths who, as any criminal intelligence analyst will tell you, are not the serious players. It is the basis for the government promise to shut down Mosques, Islamic bookshops and community centres. It places the blame for the 7 July bombings squarely at the door of Islam. It involves telling Asian youth, repeatedly, that – contrary to the Race Relations Act – they can and should be expected to be disproportionately stop-and-searched. It

Ben Hayes

involves citizenship tests and an 'integration commission' based on the premise of assimilate or leave. All of this justified with the chilling claim that 'multiculturalism is dead'.

Groundhog day

The best intelligence (again, as every intelligence analyst will tell you) is human intelligence. It is for this reason that former employees of the security services have recently been queuing up to voice their concern that the conduct of the domestic 'war on terrorism' is jeopardising the flow of intelligence from the Muslim community. They know very well that Bloody Sunday, internment and 'shoot-to-kill' united the catholic community behind the IRA and led men to enlist in their hundreds. Of course, communities in Britain will never unite behind al-Qaeda, but every time police officers are racist toward Asian youth, every time a house or Mosque is unjustly raided, and every time Islam is demonised by the government – genuine counter-terrorism is undermined while the likelihood that the terrible events of 7 July will be repeated increases.

Anyone who has thought critically about the development of the UK criminal justice system in recent times will see the parallels between the evolution of the 'war on terrorism', the 'war on drugs' and the unspoken 'wars' on other crimes such as 'illegal immigration' and, more recently, the war on 'anti-social' behaviour[22]. In each case the principle is that these social phenomena can only be solved by increased policing and punishment. In each case we have seen the creation of a shadow criminal justice system (with the arguable exception of the 'war on drugs', where we see instead a global enforcement regime) and in each case there is no attempt (or comparatively only very limited resources) to address the 'root causes'. As a result all these 'problems' are worsening because the current government is unable to countenance anything other than the increasing use of force in pursuit of the same discredited course of action. Repressive laws, more prisons, more criminals (less liberty, less security).

A great British export

For those of us who care about the preservation of civil liberties and democracy in Britain the domestic assault on the criminal justice system is only half the problem. 'Osama Bin Laden has done more for security cooperation in the EU than Jean Monet', to use the particularly crude words of one European Commissioner. The

European Union, like the British state, is taking liberties at an alarming rate.

At the heart of the EU's counter-terrorism policy is the 2002 Framework Decision on terrorism which means that all EU member states now share a common definition of terrorism that could be applied to almost any act of violence. This despite the fact that many of them have never experienced 'terrorism'. The hastily agreed Framework Decision on the European Arrest Warrant (also 2002) ushered in a new fast-track extradition system at the expense of procedural safeguards for suspects, including the possibility for their lawyer to contest the allegations against them in domestic court.

It is therefore particularly galling when Tony Blair announced, in the wake of the July 7 bombings, that 'cases such as Rashid Ramda wanted for the Paris metro bombing ten years ago and who is still in the UK' are 'completely unacceptable', we 'will set a maximum time limit for all future cases involving terrorism'[23]. The real reason Mr. Ramda is still here is that the Home Office has taken five years to make a decision on the case. As for the proposed time limits, the EU Arrest Warrant legislation has already set a 60 day deadline and since it entered force UK procedures now last a mere 17. It is sheer nonsense to suggest that the rules could possibly be tightened any further.

Then there are the four EU treaties with the United States, on mutual legal assistance, extradition, Europol and Passenger Name Record (PNR) data – all of which were agreed with no parliamentary debate. All of these treaties give US authorities *de facto* powers over EU citizens at the expense of the protection of the European Convention on Human Rights. The passenger name record treaty means that the US authorities now have direct access to airline passenger reservation databases in Europe (something many domestic EU police forces did not have). Encouraged by this agreement, the EU has agreed its own passenger name record system that will lead to the profiling of all air travellers into, out of, and across the EU.[24]

The EU has also agreed that every passport holder, every legally resident third-country national, every visa applicant and every refugee in the EU will be fingerprinted and their prints and personal data will be held in first national, then in EU-wide police databases. This legislation is behind the drive for mandatory fingerprinting in the UK and part of the reason that from late next year you will have to go to an 'enrolment centre', be photographed, fingerprinted and possibly interviewed in order to renew your passport. Faced with this reality, how will the public react? The prospect that this unprecedented invasion of privacy will pass unopposed is testimony to a slide toward authoritarianism, or 'democratic authoritarianism' as it has been called.

The same can be said of two further proposals. First, the long-standing EU proposals to introduce obligations on all service providers to preserve all telecommunications traffic data – including all call records, internet usage and mobile phone location data – must for at least one year for any law enforcement purpose. Second, the latest proposals that all police information held by one member state should be available to law enforcement agencies in all the others – the so-called 'principle of availability'.

'Policy laundering' and 'softening-up'

There is an implicit link between developments in the UK and developments in the EU, and that link is the UK government. Its permanent representatives in Brussels are engaged, shamelessly, in what is called 'policy laundering'. This means pushing authoritarian measures at the EU level and then, once they are adopted, telling the UK parliament and the public that it has no choice but to implement these measures to meet our obligations under international law.

Another approach that has been swallowed by the London and Brussels parliaments is 'softening-up', described here by Seamus Milne:

> *As negotiating tactics go, it's a pretty transparent one – but it still seems to work every time in British politics. The government has a policy it knows will arouse a blizzard of controversy. So it starts out with a maximalist, even outlandish, version. When that is predictably greeted with outrage, it retreats crab-like to its core position – and the final outcome is then accepted with relief that the government has compromised. But the net effect is to drive through measures that might have been thrown out without the softening-up process.*[25]

Exactly the same thing happens in the EU, but with much less controversy, as few understand what is being decided. As a consequence the European Union is starting to display some of the worst excesses of the Cold War era: the mandatory surveillance of communications, the surveillance and restriction of movement, and mandatory population registers and security files (not to mention central planning). At the same time, most EU member states are complicit in the construction of a US-constructed global gulag that stretches from the detention centres and airstrips of Europe to Diego Garcia, across Afghanistan and Iraq, through a host of repressive regimes and on to Guantanamo Bay.

Positive demands

The defence of civil liberties and democracy requires that positive demands are placed on the agenda. But it is no longer sufficient to simply demand that security and terrorism policy 'respect' human rights and other democratic standards because 'the rules of the game' are changing. It is now necessary to undo the damage already done in the name of the 'war on terror' and redraw the 'line in the sand' that the European Convention on Human Rights is meant to represent.

In the wake of atrocities like the July 7 bombings (and there will surely be more) we should be asking not what new powers the police and security services require, but if they are using their existing powers properly. 'Intelligence failures' and the 'shooting-to-kill' of Jean Charles de Menezes clearly suggest otherwise. The British government must be held to account – over the conduct of the 'war on terror' at home, over the Iraq war, and over the authoritarian trajectory of the European Union.

Ben Hayes is a researcher with Statewatch and joint coordinator of the European Civil Liberties Network.

Footnotes

1 Speech by Charles Clarke, 7 September 2005, full-text available at: http://www.statewatch.org/news/2005/sep/03clarke.htm.

2 Hillyard, P. & Percy-Smith, J. (1988) The coercive state: the decline of democracy in Britain (London: Fontana)

3 'The Convention was drafted in the immediate aftermath of the bloodiest, most destructive war the world has ever seen. It is not a luxury for times of peace, but a necessity to prevent tyranny and conflict.' Council of Europe Parliamentary Assembly Communication Unit, Press Release, 9 September 2005: http://www.statewatch.org/news/2005/sep/04coe-clarke.htm

4 Note that Mr. Clarke makes no mention of the right to a fair trial or the ban on torture and inhuman or degrading treatment.

5 The difficulty in accessing computer data is one of the reasons put forward by the police for extending detention without charge for terrorist suspects to three months.

6 See Paddy Hillyard's essay in this collection.

7 'Damage to the mental health of Belmarsh prisoners detained under the 2001 Anti-Terrorism legislation,' October 2004:
http://www.statewatch.org/news/2004/nov/belmarsh-mh.pdf

8 'A stampede against justice', Gareth Peirce, Guardian, 8 March 2005.

9 This has not prevented government lawyers making such claims.

10 See for example 'U.S.-Held Prisoners Transferred Abroad Subjected to Torture', Michael Ratner and Scott Harris, Between the Lines, 22 February 2005:
http://www.zmag.org/content/print_article.cfm?itemID=7292&sectionID=40

11 'This covert experiment in injustice', Gareth Peirce, Guardian, 4 February 2004.

12 Note that the EU and UN also have 'terrorist lists', criminalising hundreds of groups and individuals, see Statewatch's terrorist list site:
http://www.statewatch.org/terrorlists/terrorlists.html

13 Cited by Seamus Milne, 'This law won't fight terror – it is an incitement to terrorism', Guardian, 13 October 2005.

14 See 'Terrorising the rule of law: the policy and practice of proscription', Ben Hayes (2005), available on Statewatch's terrorist list site (see note 12, above).

15 Home Office consultation document, 5 July 2005:
http://www.statewatch.org/news/2005/aug/ukdeportation.pdf

16 BBC, 16 October 2005.

17 See http://www.statewatch.org/news/2005/apr/ukstop-and-search-2005.pdf.

18 See http://www.parliament-square.org.uk/about.html.

19 See http://www.statewatch.org/news/2003/jul/25ukus.htm.

20 Repeated surveys show that a clear majority of the UK public believe in this link and surely no-one who has seen the video made by Siddique Khan can dispute this:
http://english.aljazeera.net/NR/exeres/B22D0ADF-D0EB-4DC0-9C6E-7671F19CD589.htm.

21 Speech by Tony Blair to Labour party national conference, July 2005.

22 See Max Rowlands' essay in this collection.

23 Statement by Tony Blair, 5 August 2005,
http://www.statewatch.org/news/2005/aug/02pm-terrorstatement.htm.

24 See 'The emergence of a global infrastructure for mass registration and surveillance', ICAMS report (2005), http://www.i-cams.org/.

25 See note 13, above.

8

What's wrong with Europe?

Gus Hosein

As a North-American in Europe I often find myself having to defend the indefensible. Frequently, even amongst colleagues and friends, I am called on to defend the American response to terrorism – the USA-PATRIOT Act, extraordinary rendition, Bagram and Guantanamo Bay prison camps, torture.

But so much is going wrong in Europe itself yet so long as Europeans can point to the problematic measures in the US then no one is noticing that the European system isn't working that well either.

To be honest there are days where I despair for civil liberties outside of the US Don't get me wrong: I'm not some 'rah rah America is great' person. I am no fan of a number of policy initiatives emerging from the US since the 1990s. And of course there is the litany of legislation that deals with terrorism: USA-PATRIOT, Enhanced Border and Visa Security Reform Act, a variety of intelligence reform and homeland security legislation, and the REAL-ID Act to name but a few. All in their own ways chip away at civil liberties and enhance surveillance powers. And there is an equally bad list of policy initiatives: US-VISIT, Total Information Awareness, Computer Assisted Passenger Pre-Screening System, Secure Flight, TIPS, MATRIX, and countless other programmes and technologies that were proposed over the years.

At cocktail parties across Europe I overhear conversations about these awful programmes, practices and policies and I am expected to bow my head in shame. Indeed I do, but I do not despair about the US. In the US there are institutions, agencies and organisations at work who are trying to minimise and fix the problems that are arising.

While my head is bowed with shame I usually grit my teeth and try to resist doing what inevitably happens: I lash out. And you, the reader, will have to bear with me as I lash out on paper: Europe is heading quickly into a legal abyss of fear and indifference.

Europe's fading culture of rights

One of the largest differences between the US and European public discourses is the lack of adequate scrutiny of the police actions by the state. This was not always so; for instance in the 1980s there were public demonstrations in the Netherlands protesting against the census. But we have not seen such public demonstrations lately against police powers in Europe; in fact most public demonstrations are usually in response, again, to the actions of America.

I am going to be a bit shrewd and blame the lack of public attention to civil liberties on the perception of international institutions. In the current debate in the UK on greater anti-terrorism powers we are told that the greatest civil liberty is the right to life; and that the European Convention on Human Rights is getting in the way of the Government's attempts to ensure that 'most basic civil liberty'. This is a dangerous logic. It is most dangerous because it creates a false conflict between the great UK Government as it tries to protect the lives of Britons and the Convention that seeks to impose death and destruction upon Britain. And the public appears to believe it. By implementing the Convention into British law in 1998 under the Human Rights Act, politicians have created an external outlet for blame. On top of that, trying to find justice within the Convention process requires going all the way to the European Court of Human Rights, in Strasbourg. This process takes much patience and funding.

A similar situation arises in the regulatory regime for protecting personal data. For a long time Europeans have mocked the Americans for lacking an appropriate privacy-protection regime; the EU has a strong regime in the 1995 Directive on the protection of personal data in both the public and private sectors, while the US only has such a law protecting the use of personal information in the public sector. Consistent surveys of the American people show that the vast majority are concerned with the use of personal data by both industry and government.

In Europe there seems to be a complacency on the protection of personal data. There are no equivalent surveys. There is little public discussion on privacy. Instead regulators are entrusted and references to the 1995 Directive are considered sufficient. When the EU moved to transform privacy rules in order to enable communications surveillance the response from the general public was mute. Little debate occurred in the public domain because the decision was made at the EU and not in Member States, and also because the argument that prevailed in what little debate that was held was that if you have nothing to hide then you have nothing to fear. If such a proposal for indiscriminate surveillance was made in the US there would be massive public outcry. To date the only significant outcry has emerged from what few non-governmental organisations there are, from some public regulators, the telecommunications industry and select European Parliamentarians.

There is no daily discussion of constitutional rights and values in European societies and this can be attributed to the fact that these are alien concepts. Data protection rules are EU-based and make us complacent while we rely on the law and regulators to protect our interests; and civil liberties are hardly protected by the European Convention on Human Rights even as a false dichotomy is created to place blame on the Convention whenever a Government wishes to introduce problematic laws.

What is most lacking in Europe is the culture of rights. In the US there is certainly public support for problematic laws but there is also the public discussion on rights and safeguards, innumerable court cases brought against the Federal Government, laws introduced to minimise intrusions upon the private lives of individuals, and countless studies conducted to point out troubles and flaws. Towns have even passed ordinances calling for refusals to comply with Federal agents using powers under the USA-PATRIOT Act. The sum of all of these actions is the constitution of the open society: people acting in order to question Government policy. In the US not only do the avenues for such questions exist, but you have people pursuing them because of the culture of rights. In Europe there is a lack of such impetus to pursue these causes and I put this down to a lack of culture. (I can already hear the 'GASP' sounds as the reader hears an American accuse the Europeans of lacking culture!) Of course this is a gross generalisation. In the UK there are public demonstrations against detention powers; Britons do feel as though there is something 'un-British' about ID cards, restrictions on habeas corpus, amongst other measures introduced recently. But there is no denying that there is a significant difference to the public responses to the UK Government's policies than to the US Government's policies.

The lack of culture hurts the law
While Europe rests on its laurels of having created legal regimes such as the Council of Europe's European Convention on Human Rights and the EU's Data Protection Directive, many of the promised rights and protections are being eroded not only by Government policies but also by the lack of a strong rights culture. It is not enough to claim privacy as a constitutional right, as essential to democracy, and to

leave it at that, hoping that no further incursions will arise. No constitutional right, nor any moral right for that matter, is absolute.

Within the European Convention on Human Rights, the right to privacy is 'balanced' against many other considerations, on the following condition developed by the European Court of Human Rights: intrusions on privacy must be considered necessary in a democratic society and thus they must be deemed proportionate.

Society's attitudes thus become the barometer of privacy as a fundamental right. What is 'proportionate' and 'reasonable' is unclear. There was a time when we thought that capital and corporal punishment were reasonable and proportionate when the crimes were severe enough or the public wanted vengeance, retribution, and entertainment. Generally, this is no longer the case. But there was also a time when we believed that national databases were problematic, that mass surveillance of communications was disproportionate and unreasonable. Yet we now see these systems and practices spreading.

In December 2004 the EU established a rule that would require all European citizens to have their fingerprints compulsorily taken in order to get a passport. These fingerprints will then be verified at border entry points in the EU and, probably, while abroad. This will lead to the collection of fingerprints of 450 million individuals. As Europeans grow more accustomed to submitting their fingerprints for access to borders they are less likely to be offended when their own home governments require their fingerprints for more general purposes.

Previously we collected fingerprints of criminals, or collected information on suspects; now European societies seem less obsessed with due process, and many argue that they are willing to forgo liberty in the name of security. Some schools in the UK are collecting fingerprints from children when they borrow library books; the public outcry was again minimal and the privacy regulator even acquiesced to this collection. In the US when a school began using radio-ID tags on students it was national, and even international news and the school was embarrassed into halting the programme. As a result in the US students are learning that they must not be tagged and US society and thus US law is likely to see this as disproportionate. In the UK where fingerprinting is taking place in libraries, and across the EU where Governments will hold the fingerprints of all residents, it is likely that though there may be initial resentment, with time this will be seen as acceptable, reasonable, and proportionate. And when even greater intrusions are incurred, the Courts will say that people were willing to accept fingerprinting in schools and at borders, so subsequent policies will not be seen as unreasonable.

Five years ago we would never have pursued many of these policies and systems. I now worry most about what will happen five years from now, looking back and looking forward: what will we think is reasonable, proportionate, and necessary in a democratic society when we have given up so much already with such little struggle?

Moving on

As someone who works in what is called the 'civil society'-sector in Europe I am amazed whenever I look at the differences between the US and Europe. In the US there are countless non-governmental organizations that are well funded on just about any and every topic area. I wouldn't be surprised if there was a well funded NGO on the protection of rights of rare moss in forests of north-western states of Oregon and Washington. In Europe the landscape is dismal. And this is reflected in contemporary civil liberties struggles.

Whenever a new law is passed in the US that tries to regulate free expression there is usually a mad rush by policy experts, law organisations, civil liberties organisations, and other institutions to take the case to the Courts. Arguably the perception in the US is that this is the moment at which the true debate begins because there is a lack of trust in the legislative process.

In Europe, once a law is passed this is usually the end of the debate. The actors and resources required to take the case further are too few and too far between.

My friends and colleagues across Europe may not appreciate my characterisation of European civil society organisations and I welcome their comments. It is my belief that Europe is failing to establish adequate safeguards on the ever-increasing powers of the state because Europe relies on external institutions and lacks a culture of rights. With these two weaknesses there is a lack of civil society participation and as a result we lack the ability and resources to properly conduct campaigns and take policies further when politics fails.

And politics is failing at an increasing rate. Many of our most intrusive laws are not being decided within national legislatures but are now being established and agreed upon at international institutions. This is the act of 'policy laundering', where national executives seek laws internationally so as to bring them back to national parliaments as an 'international obligation'. At these international institutions there is limited debate and practically no oversight, particularly on policing measures.

Policy laundering is far too commonplace in Europe. Governments are seeking a variety of policies through the various European inter-governmental institutions, such as the European Union and the Council of Europe. Fingerprint databases, trans-border sharing of data for policing, communications surveillance, and immigration policies are only some of the policies being decided outside of national scrutiny.

So my European colleagues may not appreciate my characterisation of European civil society organisations, but even if we were to agree that some NGOs have a significant presence in their own countries dealing with their own governments' policies, these same NGOs are not particularly adept at dealing with these international institutions.[1] So as policy-making moves international, civil society in Europe is failing even more so.

This is why the European Civil Liberties Network is so essential. The pooling of intellectual and strategic capacities from NGOs across Europe is an absolute necessity whilst Governments co-operate on establishing invasive policies in unaccountable circumstances. High profile and necessary action to question problematic policies and appeal to legal relief are essential for the preservation, maintenance and enhancement of a culture of civil liberties in Europe.

As ever, resources remain a significant challenge and this is where I am sceptical. There are so many policies, so many institutions, so many forums and yet so few members of civil society with so little funding and capacity to counter what is going on. A radical shift in European civil society funding is perhaps needed; otherwise it will continue to be an embarrassment in comparison to the US landscape. And so long as that continues it is likely that European civil liberties and political discourse are also likely to be the butt of my jokes and the continued cause of my despair.

Gus Hosein is a Senior Fellow with Privacy International where he directs the Terrorism in the Open Society programme. He is a Visiting Fellow in the Department of Information Systems at the London School of Economics and Political Science.

Footnote
1 There are of course honourable exceptions like *Statewatch* which has worked at the European level since its formation in 1991.

9

Lampedusa – a test case for the subcontracting of EU border controls

Lorenzo Trucco

The culture of human rights probably represents the only authentic European wealth: unfortunately, the current situation places its effective implementation in danger, and the risk of a considerable number of people not having access to fundamental rights is growing.

From this perspective, the situation of migrants and, even more so, asylum seekers gives rise to serious concern in Europe, and future prospects are even more worrying. The issue of 'security' and the fight against terrorism are relentlessly lowering the minimum threshold of guarantees concerning fundamental freedoms, building up an ever-higher barrier between Europe and a mass of desperate people who, for numerous reasons, such as terrible conflicts, unbearable conditions of poverty or the destruction of the most elementary human rights, look to the European continent in the hope of finding better conditions for their existence. The dramatic images of the 'assault' at the fences of the Spanish enclaves of Ceuta and Melilla in North Africa are incredibly symbolic of the intolerable closure of Europe and cannot fail to make the blood of any democratic soul boil up in disdain.

It is inconceivable that the only answer that Europe and the European states are capable of mustering is merely in terms of repression and a further tightening of measures for removal.

And, particularly with regards to asylum seekers, we are witnessing an incredible paradox: on the one hand we have a series of fundamental conventions on human rights which reaffirm undeniable principles of care and assistance; while on the other, the procedural systems adopted by states appear to have been drawn up precisely to nullify their effectiveness, as if the culture of human rights were an annoying burden and, thus, would best be confined to a purely theoretical sphere.

At the present time, the situation in Italy is worse than ever. The changes that have been introduced into the basic law on migration by the so-called Bossi-Fini law (L. 189/2002), which was relentlessly pursued by the xenophobic Lega Nord party as well as by the right-wing government, have treated expulsion as the only means of governing the phenomenon of immigration. Thus, the law envisages several forms of immediate expulsion from the territory (i.e. loss of employment gives rise to the failure to renew a residence permit, apart from a brief six-month period, after which the foreigner is immediately expelled from the territory), detention centres (so-called CPTs) for individuals who are awaiting the execution of their expulsion, and new criminal offences that are subject to extremely heavy punishment for people who, having received the order to abandon the territory of the state within five days, do not comply with the order, and so on.

The dramatic attacks in London in 2005 immediately led to the introduction in Italian legislation of a new form of expulsion, envisaged in the so-called Pisanu decree, named after the interior minister. This norm allows (and, in fact, it has already been used) the immediate expulsion by the minister or prefetto (local police chief) of a person who 'may, in any way, assist terrorist organisations or activities'. Against this measure, only an appeal before the *Tribunale Amministrativo Regionale* (Regional Administrative Court) is allowed, limited to considerations about the legal procedure. Any possibility of the expulsion being suspended (explicitly a test case for the subcontracting of EU border controls) is excluded. It is obvious that in this way measures adopted by the police are withheld from any form of judicial oversight. Likewise, the new law in the field of asylum envisages fast-track procedures and the detention of the asylum seeker, almost in the totality of cases, in 'identification centres' set up specifically for this purpose, which lack any form of judicial control.

In reality, the central problem continues to be that of effective access to the proceedings. In fact, that is a moment when the asylum seeker is especially alone, without knowing his or her rights, while the discretionary powers of the border police to either consider them an illegal migrant or an asylum seeker and, consequently, to allow them to undergo proceedings, essentially, are not subject to any controls.

The situation is dramatic for those people who disembark on the Italian coasts, and particularly in the Sea of Sicily: from this perspective, the case of the island of Lampedusa takes on an increasingly symbolic character.

Lampedusa is a small island that lies far to the south of Sicily, a real paradise for tourists which, however, is becoming hell-like for thousands of desperate people who try to reach European territory.

Particularly in recent times, as a result of the dramatic conditions in which countries in the sub-Saharan band lie, and of conflict in the Horn of Africa, masses of boat-people who have experienced incredible vexation attempt the crossing of the Mediterranean. The shipwrecks are extremely numerous and that part of the sea has, by now, turned into an enormous cemetery, in the midst of a far from blameless silence of the civilised European community.

However, the future that the 'lucky ones' who manage to reach the island face is laden with hardship. The arrivals constantly follow each other, in spite of agreements that have been reached, for this purpose, between Italy and Libya, with the goal of preventing the persistence of this phenomenon.

During the first week of 2004, the Italian authorities directly deported to Libya over 1,500 people who had fled their countries and had disembarked in Lampedusa. Without even trying to hide the fact from public opinion, the Berlusconi government organised several flights using special planes to carry the foreigners back to Libyan territory.

The violation of the general principles of the Geneva Convention on refugees and of the Convention on Human Rights is blatant, and this is also the case in relation to the carrying out of collective expulsions: these removals took place without any control by judicial authorities, even though it is required by the basic law on immigration. The individuals who had disembarked have been treated as ordinary irregular migrants, in spite of the fact that many of them came for sub-Saharan areas and from the Horn of Africa.

In spite of the vibrant protests by numerous NGOs, the Italian government relentlessly continued its policy and in March 2005, following another series of large-scale arrivals, after a few days detention in the detention centre in Lampedusa, it organised several more deportation flights to Libya.

The situation reached such dramatic peaks that some NGOs presented a complaint to the European Commission against the Italian government. The Commission said it had no competence to intervene, even though, in the European Parliament, a motion to condemn the actions of the Italian government was agreed. Moreover, in the month of May the European Court of Human Rights in Strasbourg suspended, using an urgent procedure, the expulsion of eleven people who had left their countries and had managed, in spite of thousands of difficulties, to file these appeals.

One of the decisive problems is the extreme difficulty for someone to get in contact with the people inside the centre: the conditions of complete isolation make a real control over the actions of the police forces impossible. And in spite of the parliamentary questions asked from the ranks of the opposition, the government has always answered evasively, denying any responsibility.

Even from a strictly legal perspective, the absence of a means of appeal to suspend the removals renders the effectiveness of the work of the defence absolutely in vain, because it is obvious that once the expulsion has been carried out, the possible forms of appeal remain on a purely theoretical footing. The seriousness of the situation is all the more dramatic as a result of the fact that the removal has been executed, as mentioned above, with flights to return into Libyan territory. In April 2005, the report of a technical mission carried out by the European Commission in Libya in relation to the phenomenon of illegal immigration was published: even though it was an official mission and, therefore, any element of surprise was lacking, some of the points of this document are particularly significant. The mission, which took place over the end of November and the start of December 2004, firstly highlights that Libya has not adhered to the Geneva Convention on refugees nor to the Protocol of 1967, having only ratified the Organisation of African States Convention and that, in spite of the fact that the Libyan Constitution envisages a sort of protection for refugees, in reality there is no administrative body that is responsible for this problem, nor does the United Nations High Commissioner for Refugees have any powers to enter the detention camps.

The mission has been able to visit the detention centres, but expressly stresses that 'no information on specific procedures and criteria for detaining individuals was provided by the Libyan authorities', and that 'many of the illegal immigrants met in the centres appear to have been arrested on a random basis'.

The centres for long-term detention, according to the Commission, 'can be assimilated to prisons' and in many cases nourishment for detainees is limited to bread and water.

It is striking to note that none of the detainees who were spoken to had a minimum understanding of how long their detention would last, nor had they ever been given any information on the applicable legal procedures, while on the other hand the report also highlights that the Libyan authorities themselves had been rather evasive about this point.

Due to its position in the Mediterranean, Italy specifically stipulated a bilateral agreement with Libya in 2000 to combat terrorism, organised crime, drug trafficking and illegal immigration: in particular, concerning this last issue, from 2003 a 'permanent liaison' has been operative between the two countries. The report confirms that Italy has financed a programme of repatriation flights from Libya to the countries of origin (including, for example, Eritrea), as well as funding, in 2003, the construction of a detention camp for illegal migrants whose construction had already started in late 2004, and 'in the financial exercise 2004-2005 a special allocation is foreseen for the development of two more camps in the south of the Country, in Kufra and Sebha'.

In 2003, it was again Italy that provided a long list of materials: and it is incredible to see that the list includes '1,000 sacks for corpses transport'. The cynical awareness of the tragedy leaves one speechless.

It is very difficult to think that what happens in Lampedusa occurs by chance: rather, it appears as though it is a kind of test for a new path in the control of migration flows and policies on asylum. In fact, the European Union has already repeatedly sent out signals looking to strip itself of any responsibility by subcontracting border controls beyond its frontiers. The policy of externalising border controls can be simplified by dividing it into two main trends: on the one hand, the installation on the other side of the European borders of transit camps or screening centres, and on the other hand, the placing of a burden on third countries for part of the European Union's policy in the field of immigration and asylum, in the framework of cooperation policy, in accordance with the principle of burden sharing and of protection in the areas closest to the regions of origin. It is obvious that with these prospects, if migrants and asylum seekers could be locked up in camps outside Europe and only afterwards, following a sort of screening, some of them were to be able to enter the Union's territory, this would mean the elimination of the forms of democratic control that still persist, even though, of course, there would be no lack of the usual 'assurances' on the maintenance of minimum standards of legal guarantees.

The official funding provided by Italy for the centres in Libya is far more than a simple sign pointing in this direction.

It is worth remembering that an equivalent situation is becoming reality in Eastern Europe, where the Ukraine has set up detention centres for migrants, in disastrous conditions, undertaking the 'dirty work' of stopping the flow of people without the burden of complying with human rights conventions.

It is also necessary to stress that in spite of agreements with the Libyan government, the arrivals in Lampedusa continue as, unfortunately, do the shipwrecks. Also, in September, dozens of migrants arriving from the Horn of Africa have died at sea, joining God knows how many more, whose name and face we don't know and haven't seen.

In September 2005, at the behest, among others, of NGOs, a delegation from the European Parliament visited Lampedusa. In spite of the fact that when it arrived, the delegation only found 11 persons in the detention centre (the maximum capacity is 190 places, but it has reached peaks of over a thousand detainees), the conclusions in the report have expressed serious concern about the expulsions that were carried out to Libya by the Italian government, stigmatising the inadequacy of the centre and the absence of transparency on the part of administrative authorities in relation to the true legal status of the persons held therein. Finally, a formal report is requested concerning the mission to Libya for the control of the detention camps.

But precisely in these early days of October 2005, a serious scandal was affecting the Lampedusa detention centre: a courageous journalist, pretending to be a refugee, was detained in the centre, and told about the incredible violations that occurred, the frightening conditions, the verbal abuse and racist acts committed by members of the police forces, all of which went on without any control by the judicial authorities.

From this point of view, the very island of Lampedusa already constitutes, through its mere distance, the difficulty of access and oversight and the free reign given to police bodies, a piece of European territory that has been 'externalised'.

On the other hand, the new proposed European Directive on minimum procedural standards in the field of asylum attempts to codify [in law] a concept of safe country of origin that is based on general assumptions, proposing the adoption of a common list, with fast-track procedures that effectively exclude the legal possibility of suspending expulsion proceedings. If they are finally approved, such norms would completely undermine the principle of *'non-refoulement'*.

It is certainly difficult to know how to react when faced with the establishment of such a system for the barbarisation of the basic principles of human freedom: maybe the knowledge, information and constant interaction between different forces that complement each other, such as lawyers, political and social subjects, and so-called civil society, can implement the forms of behaviour that are able to avert the danger of the very foundations of democratic society being uprooted, in their respective milieu.

To keep one's bearings, it is worth remembering what Norberto Bobbio, the most distinguished Italian philosopher of law, argued, namely that the true difference between a democratic and a non-democratic regime is, basically, only one: while the latter is an 'exclusive' kind of regime, a democratic regime, on the contrary, is of an 'inclusive' type, meaning that it leans towards the inclusion of all individuals in the enjoyment of fundamental rights.

Lorenzo Trucco is president of A.S.G.I. (Associazione Studi Giuridici sull'Immigrazione).

[translation by Yasha Maccanico]

10

'Speech crime' and deportation

Liz Fekete

In early 2005, the Institute of Race Relations' European Race Audit (ERA) conducted research into the ways in which the definition of terrorism was being extended in a number of European countries to include 'speech crimes' and how that then impacted on Muslims and foreign nationals within the European Union. The findings of that research were released shortly after the London bombings of 7th July 2005. Since then, the debate over 'speech crimes' has intensified, with several European countries, including France, Germany and Italy, citing the London bombings to justify further counter-terror measures and amendments to immigration laws. The UK government, for its part, has introduced a new anti-terrorist act criminalising any speech that glorifies terrorism.

While the UK legislation is deeply disturbing, most attempts to outlaw speech have come not from primary legislation of this sort, but through little-known and less keenly observed administrative measures and reforms to immigration law.

Even prior to 7th July, immigration reforms had been introduced which built in to citizenship and residence rights measures which constrain freedom of speech. If those constraining measures are breached the punishment could be deportation. There can be no reasonable objection to the deportation of a foreign national who incites violence and hatred, if a court rules that deportation is a proportionate response to that crime and if the deportation is in line with international law (in particular, the provision that no-one should be sent back to countries that practise torture, the death penalty or other degrading treatment or punishment). What is of concern, however, is the lack of transparency in the deportation procedure which evades due process.

By July 2005, the European Race Audit had analysed nineteen instances in which attempts have been made in France, Germany, Italy, Poland and the Netherlands to fast-track national security deportations utilising immigration laws. All the cases involve Muslims, none of whom has been formally accused of involvement in any terrorist offence. Thirteen of the cases involve Muslim clerics or religious leaders who have been deported, or threatened with deportation, because they have made statements that are alleged to be anti-western, unpatriotic and against democratic rights. Most of those deported are long-term European residents, who could have been charged under existing public order laws.

Between July and October 2005, there have been further deportations of long-term European residents, principally in France where interior minister Sarkozy, in the light of the London bombings, launched a major operation to track down 'radicalising elements', pledged 'zero tolerance' for Muslim leaders who encourage attacks and announced plans to expel more than ten radical Islamists 'identified for promoting radical Islamist talk'.[1] As in France, this situation extends to Bavaria, Germany, where the authorities claim to have deported fourteen Muslim imams between November 2004 and July 2005.[2]

Reforms to immigration law
When anti-terrorist laws are grafted onto immigration law the normal checks and balances are not available. There is no duty of disclosure, no legal aid available to the accused, and none of the safeguards provided under criminal law.

In Summer 2004, France, Germany and Spain brought in significant changes to immigration and aliens' legislation so as to make it easier to deport foreigners even if the authorities had not accused them of any terrorist offence. The London bombings brought a further review of these procedures not only in France (see above) but in Italy where a new anti-terrorist law passed in August 2005 grants executive authorities (ie local police chiefs as opposed to judges) the power to expel legal residents from Italy on prima facie evidence that the persons pose a security threat. In the UK, the home secretary, in outlining new guidelines for deportation, has specified a list of unacceptable behaviour which will in future define the basis of immigration law deportations on the ground that the person's presence in the UK is 'not conducive to the public good'. Already, following the killing of Theo van Gogh in November 2004, the Dutch government had announced that it would introduce new measures to deal with Muslim clerics who preached hate. In addition, both Germany and the UK had altered their immigration laws enabling them to revoke citizenship from naturalised citizens deemed a public order threat. In the UK, prior to 7th July, this only applied to naturalised citizens with dual nationality, but new proposals now extend this to any naturalised citizen engaged in extremism. In France, the interior ministry has stated that it would have, in the light of the London bombings, 'no problem' deporting Muslims who inflame anti-western feeling even if they were French citizens'.[3] 'I am going to launch proceedings to deprive French imams who preach violence and fundamentalism of their French nationality; systematically expel those who do not respect our values and are not French; and step up monitoring of places of worship where extremist activities have taken root', announced interior minister Sarkozy.[4]

While the spur to such 'reforms' was different in each country (as outlined below), the legislation is remarkably similar in that it is not aimed at those accused of any specific terrorist offence or ordinary crime, but at those who have expressed opinions which can be interpreted as pro-violence, anti-western, illiberal or even simply offensive. In this way, then, the definition of terrorism is being extended to include 'speech crimes'. Such a radical departure is backed by the May 2005 Council of Europe convention on the prevention of terrorism. This requires *inter alia* state parties to criminalise direct and indirect public provocation of terrorism, recruitment and training for terrorism, and to either try or extradite persons accused of such crimes. The convention was agreed despite concerns from the Parliamentary Assembly and the Commissioner for Human Rights of the Council of Europe that the formulation could lead to an erosion of the rights to freedom of expression and freedom of association.

The French government has amended the 1945 foreigners law (which allowed for the expulsion 'in absolute emergency' of any foreigner deemed a threat to the security of the state or public safety) to include any foreigner who commits 'acts of explicit and deliberate provocation or discrimination, hatred or violence against a particular person or a group of people'.[5] The wording of the law was greeted with concern by Socialists and Communists who opposed it on the grounds that it was so vague that it could be used as a pretext to expel foreigners for a range of offences unrelated to the original intention of the Bill. The new German immigration law, which took effect on 1 January 2005, simplifies the procedure for the expulsion of foreigners who can now be expelled not just for any proven wrong-doing, but if there is an 'evidence-based threat prognosis'.[6] Proof that someone committed a crime is not needed. Again, civil libertarians criticised the vagueness of the law, pointing out that it provided no clear definition of a 'suspect' and that an expulsion order might be based on little more than 'speculation' or 'premonition'. Additional measures to revoke citizenship from naturalised citizens linked to 'unconstitutional organisations' have also been introduced. The Spanish reform enables the state to deport foreigners, including long-term residents, on the basis of suspicion that an outrage may be committed in the future against the security of the state. (There are no judicial controls over who is deported, and the state is under no obligation to furnish evidence against the accused). As previously mentioned, in the UK the post-7th July guidelines for the deportation of foreign nationals who pose a national security threat, creates a list of unacceptable behaviour which targets any foreign born national: writing, producing, publishing or distributing material, public speaking including preaching, running a website; or using a position of responsibility such as teacher, community or youth leader to express views which foment, justify or glorify terrorist violence in furtherance of particular beliefs; seek to provoke others to terrorist acts; foment other serious criminal activity or seek to provoke others to serious criminal acts; or foster hatred which might lead to inter-community violence in the UK. The civil liberties organisations Justice and Human Rights Watch believe this ill-defined and overbroad list of unacceptable behaviour amounts to a serious interference with the free expression rights of both foreign and UK nationals. By casting an 'unacceptably broad net' it will choke expression and, ironically, undermine the government's professed commitment to an open, pluralist and tolerant society.[7]

The 'preachers of hate'

Across Europe, immigration law amendments came after intense media speculation about the so-called 'preachers of hate'. Seventeen of the nineteen examples in our survey involve Muslim clerics or religious scholars. The UK reform of its citizenship law came in the wake of the Abu Hamza case. New measures introduced in the Netherlands following the killing of Theo van Gogh came after the Dutch security services (AIVD) described the Al Forqaan mosque in Eindhoven as one of six mosques where anti-western values were preached.[8] The French law was introduced as a response to the case of Abdelkader Bouziane, an imam who appealed against deportation to Algeria. While Norway and Switzerland have not yet amended immigration laws, xenophobic and centre-Right parties there are pressing for 'reform'. In Switzerland, Jean-René Fournier (PDC-Christian Democrat), president of the Valais cantonal government, stated that he was in favour of expelling Muslims who 'do not respect our values' which, he said, should be set out in a charter. He also wants Swiss citizenship withdrawn from 'fundamentalist Muslims'.[9] Responding to a Norwegian government White Paper on security, Progress Party leader Carl Hagen has demanded stronger measures against groups that publicly express views 'that frighten the Norwegian people'.[10]

But the country most utilising deportations via immigration reform is Germany. There, the government had been thwarted by the judiciary in its attempts to deport Metin Kaplan, the leader of the fundamentalist Caliphate State, who has already served a prison sentence in Germany for incitement to murder. The court had ruled that Kaplan's extradition to Turkey was unsafe, because evidence against him had possibly been obtained by the torture of his supporters by the Turkish police, and because he faced the threat of torture and degrading treatment if handed over to the Turkish authorities. (The German authorities finally succeeded in deporting Kaplan to Turkey in October 2004 after a higher court ruled that a written agreement obtained from the Turkish authorities would prevent him from being subjected to torture.)

Metin Kaplan's case allowed the centre-Right parties and the media to portray the Social Democrat-led-coalition government as soft on terrorism. Günther Beckstein, the Christian Social Union Bavarian interior minister, described the failure to deport Kaplan as 'one of the biggest disgraces for the secret services in years'.[11] There has also been a rash of media reports on the formation of Muslim enclaves and anti-German preaching conducted in some mosques, with calls for greater integration.[12] Beckstein, who is campaigning against Turkey's entry into the EU and has criticised Bavarian Turks for living in 'parallel societies', has stated that Germany's 'law on aliens takes too little account of our country's security situation'.[13]

The new German immigration law introduced the possibility of deporting 'intellectual incendiaries' or leaders publicly inciting hate, violence and terrorist acts. State premiers and officials do not have to seek the approval of the federal state before issuing deportation orders. This gives state premiers (such as Beckstein in Bavaria) a licence to deport aliens with virtually no judicial checks on their decisions. The state of Hessen reports that it deported ten imams in the first two weeks of February for 'preaching religious hatred'. North-Rhine Westphalia plans to deport 50 individuals, while a further twenty are under close surveillance.[14] Bavaria's Beckstein has confirmed a report in *Der Spiegel* (24.1.05) that he proposes to expel 100 Islamic extremists under operation 'Action Sweep Out' ('Aktion Kehraus').[15]

The German authorities have also been at the forefront of the campaign to introduce religious profiling across Europe in order to build up 'risk profiles' of Muslim communities and Islamic clerics in particular. Germany is not alone. A 2004 Dutch intelligence services report described Salafist mosques openly preaching anti-Western ideas as one of eight sources of threat to the Netherlands posed by 'radical Islam'.[16]

Immigration laws have always contained clauses that allowed for the deportation of foreign nationals on national security grounds. The French 1945 Foreigners Law has already been referred to. In the UK, the 1971 Immigration Act allowed for the deportation of foreign nationals if they were suspected of endangering national security or committing a serious criminal offence. Both laws avoided the normal checks and balances on the power of the state in the form of due process. What seems to be happening today, however, is an expansion of the definition of what constitutes a threat to national security. Today, espousing anti-western sentiments, questioning integration, voicing illiberal sentiments, advocating discrimination against specific groups in society, all come under the definition of a 'national security' threat, warranting deportation.

Expanding national security crimes

France has stated explicitly that reform of immigration law was necessary to deal with those who, through speech, espouse anti-western and anti-Enlightenment values, with the (then) interior minister Dominique de Villepin declaring that 'Today, one can no longer separate terrorist acts from the words that feed them'.[17] Clerics have been expelled because they are Salafists 'proselytising in favour of a radical form of Islam'. Abdelkader Yahia Cherif, an imam in Brittany was expelled to Algeria in April 2004, because he was alleged to have, amongst other things, rejoiced over the Madrid bombings. Orhan Arslan, a preacher at the An-Nour mosque in Mulhouse (Haut-Rhin) was expelled in January 2004 for 'making anti-Semitic and anti-western comments'. Similarly, Midhat Güler, director of a Paris mosque, was accused of inciting hatred of western societies and Israel in sermons and allowing Islamic newspapers that glorified jihad to be circulated in a prayer room. The deportation of Abdelkader Bouziane, the imam at the Al-Forquan mosque in the largely immigrant suburb of Vénissieux, in April 2004, came after the newspaper *Lyon Mag* published an interview with Bouziane which quoted him as saying that the Koran authorised men to beat their wives and that the stoning of women was permissible. The expulsion was justified on the grounds of 'defending crime' and 'direct provocation against the integrity of a person without leading to any effect'. Since July 7th, deportation orders seem to have got even vaguer, with little attempt to define what actual crime was commited to merit deportation. Hence, in July 2005 the crime of Reda Ameuroud, expelled to Algeria, was classified simply as one of providing an 'ideological reference point' by his 'violent and hate-filled' speeches at a radical mosque in Paris's 11th arrondisement. The deportation order against Abdallah Cam, an imam from Villeurbanne, merely stated that the imam's expulsion was 'an imperative necessary for the security of the state and the public'.[18]

In Germany, Muslim clerics are also being deported for a variety of speech crimes. In February 2005, in Bremen, a 43-year-old Egyptian imam (name unknown) was identified in the media as a 'preacher of hate'. Even though the Public Prosecutor's Office confirmed that it had no evidence upon which to base a prosecution, he was deported, it seems, because he had called on Muslims to defend their religion against the 'evils of imperialism'.[19] The Berlin constitutional court ordered that Yakup Tasci, imam of the Mevlana mosque in the Kreuzberg district, should be deported on the grounds that he represented a serious danger to public safety. It cited a public speech in which he was said to have glorified Islamic martyrs in Iraq and Jerusalem and, in the form of a poem, suggested suicide attacks in Germany.[20] Another case is that of Salem El R., the imam of the Al-Nur mosque in Berlin, who was alleged to have made inflammatory speeches in which he said 'May God protect the mujaheddin in Chechnya, Palestine and Iraq' and 'May God let a tornado sweep away the enemies of Islam, smash them and destroy them.'[21]

Dutch interior minister Rita Verdonk also wants to use immigration law to facilitate speedy deportations of 'undesirable aliens' who pose a threat to public order and national security. Three imams, who security services accuse of 'contributing to the radicalisation of Muslims in the Netherlands', 'recruiting or tolerating the recruiting of Muslims for Jihad' and 'using their sermons to urge Muslims to isolate themselves from Dutch society', have appealed against a decision to rescind their residence rights.[22] The Iskender Paso mosque in Rotterdam (not listed by the AIVD as a hotbed of terrorism) has threatened to sue *De Telegraaf* over a story that its imam had been deported for preaching hate. It seems that the person expelled was not the imam (he led Friday prayers the day after his reported expulsion), but a volunteer at the mosque who had been taken into custody for not having a valid residence permit.[23]

Litigation not expulsion

The question is whether there is credible evidence that these Muslim clerics and religious teachers posed a real threat to national security. And, if they did, was it legitimate for the state to deport them? Unfortunately, the systems that are being put into place across Europe to allow for deportations makes it impossible to answer such questions.

Another problem stems from the fact that the authorities are not suggesting that the nature of the threat these individuals posed is direct, in that they were carrying out, or preparing to carry out physical acts of violence. What they were accused of is the more indirect offence of threatening national security through inflammatory speeches and sermons. And it is because their offences related to words rather than deeds that the issue of 'credible evidence' is so crucial.

The normal solution to crimes relating to incitement would be for charges to be made under existing public order or criminal laws. But these Muslim clerics are being excluded from the ordinary rule of law and enclosed within a parallel, shadow criminal justice system that has a lower standard of proof and greater punishment for those deemed guilty. This parallel criminal justice system, to date, has only applied to Muslims. Youcef Mammery of the Marseilles Council of Muslims identifies working-class, badly-educated Muslim communities as the real target of these measures, adding that 'There are very orthodox people in all religions, who live life on the margins of modern society.'[24] The French Coalition Against Islamophobia, the Union of French Islamic Organisations, and the Human Rights League have all condemned the hot-tempered rhetoric of badly-educated Muslim clerics, but they also defend their right not to be discriminated against, and to be afforded the same access to justice as preachers from other communities. Mammery adds that 'extreme doesn't necessarily mean dangerous'. Pointing to the case of Bouziane, he said that the imam 'wasn't very clever but it wouldn't be fair to say he was dangerous'. He argues that litigation, not expulsion, is the answer to any alleged public order offences.[25]

Clerics deemed a threat to European values are denied access to the protection of the European Convention on Human Rights which guarantees the right to a fair trial; to be presumed innocent until proven guilty according to law; to be informed promptly and in detail of the nature and cause of an accusation; to examine or have examined witnesses. In France, the state issues a deportation order and the legality of that order is subsequently decided upon by an administrative tribunal (as opposed to a criminal court). Here, the evidence cited against the accused is provided either by the security services or takes the form of submissions based on, or including, newspaper articles.

The role of the media
The evidence presented often seems to be based on little more than newspaper articles which quote inflammatory (or merely offensive) statements made by the clerics or simply regurgitate the views of unnamed security sources. The clerics have no opportunity to defend themselves against any possible misrepresentation of their views. Abdelkader Yahia Cherif was accused by the French intelligence services of rejoicing over the Madrid bombings; they cited comments made during a sermon and in a newspaper interview. His lawyers dispute the allegation that he 'rejoiced' at the Madrid bombings, stating that what he actually said was that there was no 'absolute proof that Islamists were involved in either the September 11th or the March 11th attacks'.[26] Abdelkader Bouziane's lawyers challenge whether the content of a published interview (the newspaper quoted Bouziane as saying that the Koran authorised violence against women, including stoning for adultery) actually reflected his views, pointing out that the interview lasted ninety minutes, that the imam speaks poor French and that his comments were seriously distorted.[27] (The security services had also provided evidence that Bouziane, following military intervention in Iraq, called during a sermon for a jihad against American interests in France. But it should be pointed out that when sermons are delivered in Arabic, the evidence cited by the intelligence services is not direct speech but a translation.) In respect of Bouziane's views on political violence, his lawyers argued

that the *Lyon Mag* journalist accurately represented his views, quoting him as saying that he did not want 'to raise his voice, strike or attempt to assassinate anyone in order to convert people to Islam' and that 'it is a great sin to plant a bomb because Allah is angered when innocents are killed'.

In the case of the Berlin cleric Yakup Tasci, it would seem that the media actively sought a deportation order on the grounds that he was a 'preacher of hate'. For despite the earlier accusations against him (see above), the senator for internal affairs only supported Tasci's deportation for 'seriously endangering public safety and order' and placing in danger the 'peaceful coexistence between Germans and non-Germans' after a German television station had sent journalists undercover into the Berlin mosque and filmed the cleric criticising Germans for being useless and unclean. (He had suggested that Germans were dirty as they allowed sweat to gather under their armpits which they did not shave.) Lawyers for Tasci appealed on the grounds that some of the statements ascribed to him by the Aliens Office were either wrongly interpreted or taken out of context, while others were never made at all.[28]

The same factors seem to be at play in Italy where Muslims have also been deported following newspaper stories. Abdel Qader Fadlallah Mamour, an imam in Turin, was deported to Senegal hours after giving an interview to a newspaper in which he warned that if Italian troops were not pulled out of Iraq, there could be a bomb attack in Rome, and boasted knowing Osama bin Laden.[29] In April 2005, Abdul Karim al-Tibsi, a teacher of Arabic and Islam at the Islamic Centre in Rome and a member of the Union of Arab Communities in Italy, was expelled after he led prayers in memory of Sheik Ahmad Yassin, the Hamas spiritual leader assassinated by an Israeli missile attack in Palestine.[30]

Evidence based on secret intelligence
Nor does untested evidence presented by the security services really constitute 'credible evidence'. In France, administrative tribunals have not been provided with wiretap evidence, witness testimony or other material evidence to justify the deportation of the accused. Instead, evidence takes the form of confidential notes issued by the intelligence services, commonly known as '*notes blanches*' (because they are not signed or dated and do not cite sources). In the case of Abdelkader Bouziane, classified documents submitted by the interior

minister linking Bouziane to extremist groups were actually thrown out (one piece of evidence was a 'confidential note' from the intelligence services made during a sermon by the imam in November 2003) and the court ordered that Bouziane (who had already been expelled to Algeria) was free to return to France on his own volition. (He has now been expelled for a second time after the Supreme Administrative Court quashed the earlier verdict.) In the case of Midhat Güler, the only security service evidence was a *'note blanche'* which did not even implicate Güler in terrorist acts but accused him of inciting hatred of western societies and Israel in his sermons and of other vague offences. The deportation to Algeria of Yousef Mahlili, an imam from Bilbao who moved to Mourenx to preach in a town close to the French-Spanish border, was based on a security service assessment that his sermons had become increasingly radical and critical of Spain following the Spanish decision to send troops to Iraq. (The Spaniards facilitated his deportation by rescinding his residence permit.)[31] In Germany, too, it was the evidence of an agent from the Office for the Defence of the Constitution which led to the deportation of the Berlin imam Salem El R., for making inflammatory speeches. But the *Berliner Morgenpost* (10.5.05) observed that when the imam had testified in a Berlin district court in the course of a trial of alleged terrorists, he gave every impression of moderation and had also attempted to become a German citizen.

No right of appeal

A fair system would also establish a meaningful right of appeal prior to deportation, in accordance with the Universal Declaration of Human Rights and the European Convention on Human Rights which guarantee the right to effective remedy against interference with rights. The French, Italian and Dutch systems are working in such a way that the individual is deported prior to appeal. (Abdelkader Bouziane's lawyers launched a successful appeal from abroad.) Although a regional court in Lazio ruled Abdel Qader Fadlallah Mamour's deportation illegal, as he had merely expressed what amounted to 'personal views', he had already been deported to Senegal and the Italian interior minister ruled out the possibility of any return.[32] In June, the Dutch interior minister Rita Verdonk told three imams to leave the country voluntarily, or be expelled. They have a month to appeal but they cannot stay in the Netherlands pending the outcome of any appeal.[33]

The German immigration reform, which established that suspects could be expelled on the word of the interior minister alone, has set up a special panel within the Federal Administrative Court in Karlsruhe as the sole court of appeal. The German system of appeal seems to work along the lines of the Special Immigration Appeals Commission (SIAC) in the UK. Formally a 'superior court of record', SIAC is the sole court of appeal for foreigners living in Britain whom the home secretary wants to deport on national security grounds, when some of the evidence against them is considered too sensitive to be disclosed in open court. Hence, much of the SIAC proceedings are carried out in secret session. Since the Anti-Terrorism Crime and Security Act (2001) the Commission has fallen into disrepute and is regarded as little more than a 'rubber stamp' for decisions already made by the home secretary.

Guilt by association

For the security services, an indicator of 'threat' is that a suspect has associated with other suspected wrong-doers or their associates. This is very much in accord with post-September-11th counter-terrorism measures which extended the definition of terrorism from concrete acts of extreme violence to 'any form of support' for terrorism, 'active or passive'. In a court of law, the chances of a successful prosecution based on association with a suspected wrong-doer without any corroborative evidence of 'conspiracy to commit acts preparatory to violence' would surely be slim. But fast-track deportations of foreigners via immigration reform bypass the courts and due process.

It is true that an administrative tribunal can provide some checks. In the case of Abdelkader Bouziane, for instance, the French administrative tribunal refused to accept as evidence classified documents submitted by the interior minister which linked Bouziane to extremist groups. But the deportations of other Muslim clerics have been justified on the vague grounds of association with terrorists. Abdelkader Yahia Cherif, who was seeking political asylum in France at the time of his expulsion to Algeria, was accused of 'active relations with national or international Islamic movements that are in relation with organisations advocating terrorist acts'.[34]

When crimes of association are created, whole communal, friendship or political networks can become stigmatised as 'associated with terrorism'. Midhat Güler, a sewing supplies salesman and director of a Paris mosque, was accused by the security services of being an associate of the Cologne imam Metin Kaplan, and founder of the Caliphate movement in France. But his lawyers deny the accusations, saying that while Güler knew Metin Kaplan, he was merely a family friend, and Güler had no political link with him or with the Caliphate State.[35] In Bremen, an imam of Egyptian descent who had condemned the 'evils of imperialism' (see above) was accused by the security services of links with a Turkish national currently held at Guantanamo Bay and with a German-Lebanese citizen who, at the age of 17, hijacked a bus in Bremen.[36]

Residence rights curtailed

The Muslim religious leaders deported under these provisions have not come recently to Europe; nor were they, like Louis Farrakhan entering Europe from outside for a limited speaking tour. Most of the cases involve Muslims who have lived in Europe for years, decades even, and many have children born here. (Abdelkader Bouziane had lived in France for twenty-five years on a renewable residence permit; Abdallah Cam, who has four children, had lived legally in Villeurbanne for ten years; Midhat Güler had lived in France since 1976; Abdul Karimn al-Tibsi had been legally resident in Italy for 12 years.) As such they should enjoy residence rights, including freedom of speech and assembly. As such they were entitled to safeguards enshrined in the European Convention on Human Rights, which protect the right to family and private life. These state that expulsion, which separates someone from his or her family and severs links they have built up in the country of residence, must be justified by a pressing social need (ie. it must be proportionate to a legitimate aim such as protecting national security or prevention of crime or disorder). The European Court of Human Rights has in the past protected from deportation immigrants who have served prison sentences for serious crimes on the grounds that deportation would be disproportionate (a form of double punishment) and a violation of the right to family life. In the cases where Muslim clerics have been denied due process, we would never know whether the principle of 'proportionality' was adhered to.

Political pressure

Some of the other cases we have documented seem to be linked to the need to satisfy the demands of international partners in the International Coalition Against Terrorism.

Since 2001, the US has been pressing the European Commission to ease the laws on extradition of terrorist suspects and 'explore alternatives to extradition including expulsion and deportation'. Two deportations from Germany to Lebanon, and one from Germany to Jordan appear to have happened after pressure from the US and Israel. The two Lebanese men, long-term residents in Germany, were linked to Hizbollah. An unnamed representative of Hizbollah, who had lived in Germany for twenty years on a renewable residence permit, was told that he had to leave the country because he was 'a member of an organisation that supports international terrorism'.[37] (Only the military wing of Hizbollah, which had seven seats in the Lebanese parliament, was on the EU list of terrorist organisations. Nevertheless, in its latest annual report, Germany's domestic security agency cited 850 members of Hizbollah living in Germany as constituting a threat.)[38] A German court refused to countenance the unnamed man's appeal on the grounds that Hizbollah was 'waging a war with bomb attacks against Israel with inhumane brutality and against citizens'.[39] Fadi Madi, a member of the International Movement Against American and Zionist Globalisation and Supremacy, has also been deported to Lebanon following the revocation of his visa in September 2004. Madi, who was deported for his 'anti-Israel and anti-US stance', had been an organiser of a conference planned to take place in Berlin in October 2004 which the Simon Wiesenthal Centre in Israel had lobbied the German government to ban. Subsequently, an investigation was launched by the German authorities into Fadi's 'membership of questionable organisations'.[40] The final case that merits a mention involves the deportation of an unnamed Jordanian national living in North-Rhine Westphalia who was expelled on the grounds that he had formerly been head of the Al-Aksa group (as this organisation has only recently been banned it seems that the law was applied retrospectively). He was also suspected of collecting donations in Germany to support the Palestinian group Hamas and by doing so had violated Germany's 'spirit of seeking understanding among peoples'.[41]

The deportation of ten Pakistani students from Cyprus in July 2005 may well have been carried out by the Cypriot government in order to appease its US allies who had just issued a warning that foreign interests on the island could be the target for attack. There was widespread consternation when the ten young men, described by the college director as 'excellent students', were arrested and linked in the media to Al-Qaeda. But the interior minister refused to comment on the arrests, citing national security.[42]

The case of Abdul Karim al-Tibsi may have involved pressure from Algeria – another key ally in the International Coalition Against Terrorism. As previously noted, Abdul Karim al-Tibsi was deported from Italy after an Arab journalist published an article alleging he had terrorist links. (It is not unknown for the Algerian security services to spread disinformation about its dissidents via a steady trickle of accusations in the press emanating from unnamed security sources.) The deportation to Yemen of Ahmed Ammar, a student studying for a doctorate on Islamic law in Poland, may also have been ordered for political reasons. The Polish internal security agency refused to give details of Ammar's alleged crimes, save citing a general threat to national security. But Ammar contended that the deportation order was due to his opposition to the war in Iraq, and the presence of Polish troops there.

And, domestically, fast-track deportation procedures are now politically expeditious. Public criticism is mounting that Europe's new anti-terrorist laws are anti-democratic and violate international human rights standards. In the UK, criticism focused until recently on the detention without trial of foreign nationals, while in other European countries human rights groups have criticised the fact that terrorist suspects have been deported on national security grounds to countries like Egypt, Algeria, Morocco and Turkey. Such extraditions being in violation of the principle of *non-refoulement* whereby foreign nationals cannot be extradited to a state where they risk persecution, the death penalty, torture or other degrading treatment or punishment.

Extradition is a lengthy process with inbuilt legal safeguards. Crucially, it gives time for lawyers and human rights activists to challenge the state's case against the accused. But deporting someone via immigration laws removes the accused from the safeguards of the criminal justice system. It could also be argued that such deportations merely displace the problem of terrorism – for those deported for speech crimes can, if they are so inclined, go on to incite violence against western targets and western tourists abroad.

Of course, there is an apparent logic to the argument that, following the Madrid and London bombings, the pronouncements of fundamentalist Muslim clerics are so dangerous that reforms are needed to allow for deportations. But any law that discriminates between one section of citizens and another undermines democracy and can alienate the very community whose support is most vital to the stamping out of terror.

Liz Fekete is Deputy Director of the Institute of Race Relations.

Footnotes

1 *Guardian* (27 May 2005); *Agence France Presse* (19 July 2005).
2 IslamOnline (28 July 2005).
3 *Agence France Presse* (7 July 2005).
4 *Agence France Presse* (19 July 2005).
5 *Migration News Sheet* (July 2004).
6 Amnesty International, Counter-terrorism and criminal law in the EU (AI Index: IOR 61/013/2005).
7 Exclusion or Deportation from the UK on Non-Conducive Grounds: a Justice Response (Justice, August 2005). See hrw.org/english/docs/2005/08/10/uk11620.htm
8 *Expatica News* (23 February 2005).
9 *Migration News Sheet* (December 2004).
10 *Aftenposten* (17 November 2004)
11 As cited in Amnesty International, Counter-terrorism and criminal law in the EU, *ibid.*
12 *Deutsche Welle* (24 November 2004).
13 *Expatica News* (16 June 2003).
14 *IslamOnline* (16 February 2005).
15 *Reuters* (23 January 2005).
16 *Times* (24 November 2004).
17 *Wall Street Journal* (9 August 2005).
18 *International Herald Tribune* (26 July 2005); *Agence France Presse* (7 September 2005).
19 *Migration News Sheet* (March 2005).
20 *Berliner Morgenpost* (23 March 2005).
21 *Berliner Morgenpost* (10 May 2005).
22 *Migration News Sheet* (March 2005), *Expatica News* (25 February 2005).
23 Ibid.
24 *BBC News* (31 May 2005).
25 *Ibid.*
26 *Le Monde* (20 August 2004), *Guardian* (23 March 2004).
27 *Agence France Presse* (23 April 2004), *Migration News Sheet* (July 2004).
28 *Berliner Morgenpost* (23 March, 15 April 2005), *Berliner Zeitung* (16 April 2005).
29 See Anti-terrorism and human rights', European Race Bulletin (No 47, 2003).

30 *IslamOnline* (25 April 2005).
31 *Migration News Sheet* (July 2004).
32 *Migration News Sheet* (January 2005).
33 *Expatica News* (26 June 2005).
34 *Migration News Sheet* (May 2004).
35 *Migration News Sheet* (June 2004).
36 *Migration News Sheet* (March 2005).
37 *Migration News Sheet* (February 2005).
38 *Deutsche Presse Agentur* (17 May 2005).
39 *Migration News Sheet* (Feburary 2005).
40 *Deutsche Welle* (19 September 2004).
41 *Deutsche Presse Agentur* (20 May 2005).
42 *Agence France Presse* (9 July 2004).

11

EU law and family reunion: a human rights critique[1]

Steve Peers

October 3, 2005, was the deadline for EU Member States to implement the EU's new Directive on family reunion for third-country [non-EU] nationals.[2] This is an opportune time to examine EC rules on family reunion for various categories of persons, which have been criticised for racism, class bias, sex discrimination, human rights breaches, homophobia and violation of children's rights.

Taking these points in turn, although there is clearly no direct race discrimination in EC family reunion law, critics of EC family reunion law have argued that indirect race discrimination resulted from the exclusion of third-country national sponsors (and EC national sponsors who have not exercised free movement rights) from EC free movement law rules on family reunion, which only cover the family members of EU citizens who have exercised free movement rights within the EU.[3] Following the adoption of the family reunion Directive, this argument is no longer valid. However, the highly graduated distinctions between sponsors on grounds of nationality, still evident after the family reunion Directive, clearly results in indirect race discrimination, since non-EU citizens have far fewer rights to have their family members join them under the family reunion Directive than EU citizens who exercise free movement rights have according to EC free movement law. Following the classic definition of indirect discrimination, there are more white people falling within the categories of sponsors with privileged family reunion law and more non-white people falling within the non-privileged categories. The EC's Council knows this full well, otherwise it would not have believed it necessary to exempt certain immigration matters from the scope of the EC's race discrimination directive.[4] But what of the European Court of Human Rights' rejection of the race discrimination argument as regards differential family reunion rules in the Abdulaziz case, along with later rejections of arguments based on Article 14 of the European Convention on Human Rights (the non-discrimination clause) in Moustaquim and C?[5] In Abdulaziz, the Court only compared the general rules for admission to the rules applicable to those sponsors with close links to the UK. It did not examine whether the UK could have different rules for different countries. In Moustaquim and C, the Court did accept that EU Member States could not just maintain different rules regarding nationals and non-nationals, but also regarding EU citizens and non-EU citizens, at least as regards expulsion. But it should be recalled that the Court condemned nationality discrimination strongly in its Gaygusuz judgment, concerning discrimination related to social security benefits.[6] Let us examine the arguments regarding admission and expulsion in turn.

As for admission, the Court argued in Abdulaziz against a finding of race discrimination on the grounds that the UK rules restricting family reunion being attacked in that case were an attempt to restrict primary immigration. In the Court's view, they were not directly discriminatory, and could not be regarded as discriminatory merely because more non-white people were affected than white people; this was simply the consequence of more non-white people wanting to immigrate to the UK. This finding was not affected by a favourable rule for those with UK ancestry, as these were considered exceptions for the benefit of those with close links with the UK, which do not accept the tenor of the general rules. This ruling confuses the separate issue of the rules on primary immigration (not as such covered by human rights law) with the family reunion rules which fall within the scope of Article 8 of the European Convention (which enshrines the right to private life and the right to family life); surely it is not beyond the powers of any court to distinguish between these two sets of rules. The reasoning as regards indirect discrimination does not follow the usual approach, which is to examine possible justifications once a differential effect is clearly made out. Nor is it clear why a specific part of the national rule should simply be disregarded. The underlying question evaded here was why two sets of sponsors should be in a different position as regards the enjoyment of their right to family life.

A clearer answer to this question was offered in Moustaquim and C, based on the distinctions between sponsors who are home State or EC nationals on the one hand and all other sponsors on the other. Certainly there are distinctions between the sponsors, but can that justify distinctions as regards the enjoyment of family life? In Abdulaziz, the Court expressly noted that the sponsors did not have a secure right of residence in the host State. Obviously such sponsors cannot be compared with host State nationals or even EC nationals coming for a short stay, since the latter have the right to 'switch' to other free movement categories and to stay indefinitely if they meet the relevant conditions.[7] But there is far less distance between the status of long-term residents and the position of home State or EC nationals. In fact, at the 1999 Tampere European Council (summit meeting) the EU resolved to treat long-term residents the same as EC nationals 'as far as possible'. It could even be said that the EC's approach to long-term residents is part of its 'special legal order'. Alternatively, it is hard to see why the 'special legal order' criterion exists at all, unless it simply refers to the enhanced immigration status of EC national sponsors. Otherwise EU Member States would have *carte blanche* to justify any form of unequal treatment between EU and non-EU nationals as regards any of the rights in the Convention, including such matters as detention, fair trials and freedom of religion. It may even be questioned whether this concept is now implicitly overruled by the more recent judgments bringing the activity of EU Member States implementing EC law within the scope of the Convention.[8] Even if the 'special legal order' justification still exists, there is still insufficient distinction in the immigration status of EU citizens (considering that their citizenship status does not confer absolute prohibition of expulsion in all Member States) and long-term resident third-country nationals to justify any distinction as regards expulsion or admission of family members. This interpretation would also better respect the critical view of nationality discrimination expressed in Gaygusuz and Poirrez. The Strasbourg Court cannot take such a strong, principled position against nationality discrimination and at the same time shrug off any such discrimination the EC chooses to practise with the excuse that the EC is a 'special legal order'.

Next, critics argue that EC rules contain a class distinction as regards family reunion, because the sponsors must exercise an economic activity or have sufficient funds in order to exercise their rights.[9] This argument is less valid in recent years given the willingness of the Court of Justice to rule that EU citizenship confers a right to social benefits, in at least some circumstances.[10] But the focus on the particular circumstances of the citizens in these judgments and the EU Court of Justice's references to the possible legitimacy of refusing benefits in other cases suggest that citizenship still does not entail a fully-fledged right to move to another Member State and obtain social assistance from that State as a sole source of income. So there still remain distinctions based on wealth and income, even for EU citizens and their families. Taking race and class together, third-country nationals with a need for social assistance will be entirely prevented from family reunion (unlike those EC nationals with some earned income supplemented by top-up benefits), and those with irregular and unstable work will (unlike EC nationals) have difficulty qualifying for family reunion. Moreover, there is a greater risk of family reunion being terminated later for third-country nationals since access to social assistance after family members enter will more likely lead to possible termination of their reunion rights.

As for sex discrimination, critics have argued that women are vulnerable after divorce if they are not EC nationals exercising economic activities, particularly since EC free movement law refuses to recognise unpaid caring or voluntary work as 'work'.[11] In the case of EC free movement law, this objection has been answered to some extent by the Baumbast and R judgment of the Court of Justice,[12] which expressly recognises the position of carers, although certain important issues (the position following divorce from other sponsors or where children are too young for education, the status of the family members in question) are still unresolved and the case would not benefit women who do not have children to care for. Access to social security by family members has also been improved,[13] and the broader access to social assistance as a result of the case law on citizenship rights may also be relevant in such cases.

But the position of Turkish women is weaker, in that they cannot usually separate (never mind divorce) from the family they were authorised to join for three years unless they can attain worker status in their own right, unusual facts such as Eyup apply,[14] or a Baumbast and R principle, protecting the migration status of the carers of the children of former workers, applies to the EC-Turkey agreement. As for the family reunion Directive, there is a clear autonomous right to stay after a certain period but with many limits and caveats, although the EC's long-term residents' Directive has improved this situation.[15] Since there is no automatic possibility to switch to the sponsor's status, as there is for EC nationals and Turkish family members of Turkish workers, the dependence of the spouses upon the sponsor will be even further exaggerated. The Community has thus set up a graduated system of sex discrimination, with the position worsening in stages the further the sponsor and the family member gets from the EU national 'norm'.

It should not be forgotten, however, that men can face immigration difficulties, too.[16] The comparative situation of divorced men compared to divorced women has worsened following Baumbast and R, as men will rarely be able to claim the status of carer, although overall men will usually be more likely to maintain their immigration status through workforce participation given their lesser share of family responsibilities and (for third-country nationals) enhanced access by the sponsor to the labour market. Having said that, in practice a significant percentage of women exercising EC free movement rights exercise the right to participate in the workforce, although a greater percentage of them curtail such participation due to maternity.[17]

Is EC family reunion law guilty of human rights breaches, due to defining the 'family' too narrowly, or failing to recognise the humanity of former spouses after divorce?[18] On the first point, certainly the definition of 'family' in EC family reunion law is narrower than that found in human rights law, where siblings and extended relatives and particularly unmarried partners (at least where a joint child exists) are considered to be family members. But it should not be forgotten that despite this wide definition, family reunion under the European Convention is only protected in limited cases as far as admission is concerned. So the definition in EC law is more problematic when it comes to expulsion, where it is clear from European Convention on Human Rights case law that an unmarried partner has protection from expulsion, at least as a parent. Within EC free movement law, this position is unexplored, although it has been suggested above that if the partner is allowed entry, the principles in the Baumbast and R judgment would apply.[19] As for admission, it would follow from the case law of the European Court of Human Rights that the limited obligation to admit family members could also apply to unmarried partners in the right case.

Apart from the definition of 'family', the EC free movement rules and association agreement rules are in many respects more generous than the human rights rules, not just as regards the clear right of admission under the free movement rules but also as regards issues of family members' status, which are not dealt with under the European Convention on Human Rights except as regards expulsion. Even the family reunion directive goes further than the case law of the European Court of Human Rights regarding admission in some respects, although it does not fully take on board the latest case law. Similarly it does not take on board recent cases as regards expulsion and remedies, so the compatibility of the Directive with human rights law can in several respects be doubted.[20] While it might be argued that this is begging the question, since a minimum standards Directive leaves

Member States free to apply higher standards if necessary to meet their human rights obligations, it is submitted that the obligation to respect human rights based on the Convention as general principles of Community law, set out in Article 6, cannot mean that EC legislation can permit lower standards than the Convention standard even on a discretionary basis. This could lead to confusion in Member States as to which standards they must follow and surely cannot be described as 'respecting' human rights obligations.

The more fundamental problem here is not with the EC rules, but with the family reunion judgments of the Strasbourg Court. There is no justification for that Court's conservatism regarding the admission of family members as seen in the Ahmut and Gul judgments, which accepted that Member States could deny admission for children to join their parents despite sound humanitarian arguments.[21] In particular, the argument that the refusal to admit family members is not in principle an interference with family life is unsustainable. Since the Convention also requires respect for private life and includes the right to marry and found a family in Article 12, the right to respect for family life should entail an obligation in principle to accept the private decisions of families as to where to carry out family life, in particular in the case where one of the family members is a national of or a long-term resident in a European Convention on Human Rights Contracting Party. In that case, an obligation to leave that State in order to enjoy a family life would clearly entail a refusal to respect the right to private life as defined by the Court, or (in the case of nationals) a breach of the right to live in one's own country as implied by the Fourth Protocol to the Convention. This approach to the issue would still leave States the right to apply Article 8(2) of the Convention permitting limitation of Article 8 rights in the event of public security, *inter alia*, in particular cases where there is strong evidence to believe that a specific family member would commit serious crimes after admission, and would still leave States' discretion as regards primary immigration intact.

On the second argument, the failure to respect the dignity and humanity of former spouses (or potentially grown-up children, particularly if they are third-country nationals) requires a shift from a focus on the protection of family life to the protection of individuals. Certainly the failure in EC free movement law to provide expressly for the acquisition of autonomous status results in such a lack of respect.[22] It cannot be argued that the 'right to human dignity' is not recognised in EC law, as the right is expressly set out in the EU

Charter of Fundamental Rights and the Court has also explicitly accepted its existence as part of the general principles of EC law.[23] As set out above in the discussion of sex discrimination critiques, there is a limited move toward providing for autonomous status in the recent case law and legislation, but it is still ambiguous or insufficient.

As for homophobia,[24] it is true that the Court of Justice rejected in its Reed judgment in the 1980s the inclusion of any relationship outside formal marriage as a 'spousal' relationship,[25] and the more recent judgments of the Court in Grant and D v Council appear to consider that partnerships and presumably marriages between same-sex couples recognised by the law of a Member State cannot be considered as 'marriages' by EC law.[26] Here again, as in the case of race discrimination, EC discrimination law has attempted to protect immigration law against allegations of discrimination based on sexual orientation.[27] However, the Reed principle requiring equal treatment between home State national workers and EC national workers exercising free movement rights as regards entry of unmarried partners presumably applies equally to same-sex relationships between unmarried partners (or persons in a registered partnership). It is arguable that the principle applies to other categories of EC free movement law beyond the movement of workers,[28] and the principle definitely now applies in the general family reunion Directive, although only as an option for Member States. But the situation remains uncertain even for EC nationals and the option permitted Member States as regards third-country nationals leaves the position for them entirely up to national discretion. Sooner or later, the Court will be forced to choose between its support for abolishing obstacles to free movement of persons and its apparently unchangeable conservative instincts as regards same-sex and opposite-sex partners alike.

Finally, as for children, critics argue that they have not been given autonomous rights within the free movement rules of the EC.[29] But as noted above, there has been in recent case law recognition of children's autonomy at a later stage, upon entry into or graduation from vocational training.[30] The Court of Justice also implicitly accepts that secondary school pupils who move are exercising EU citizenship rights,[31] and the logic of the Baumbast and R judgment is that a parent carer and migrant worker's child are mutually dependent on each other – with the child taking a lead role in the perspective of EC free movement law. Next, the Avello judgment then expressly accepted children's status as EU citizens and their corresponding right to non-discrimination on grounds of nationality.[32] Finally, the Court of Justice confirmed that under EC free movement law, babies who are EU citizens have a right to free movement before they can even walk or crawl.[33] However, the family reunion Directive clearly treats third-country national children as secondary to sponsors, with only a limited prospect that Baumbast and R might apply to protect the carers of children, or that they might otherwise attain autonomous status. Furthermore the education and training rights in the Directive are weak and the Directive provides for no other social benefits for children as members of families.

The EU's legislators and judiciary have taken some tentative efforts to address the criticisms of EC family reunion law. It cannot now be said that third-country nationals are not covered by any EC rules, that former spouses will always face expulsion after divorce, that unmarried partners will never be successful in obtaining entry, that only the already economically successful can ever rely on free movement law or that children are fully ignored as autonomous agents by EC law. However, on many of these points, EC law still has a long way to go. As far as we know, there is still no right at present to bring unmarried partners to all Member States when exercising free movement rights, regardless of the impact on free movement law or the indirect discrimination on grounds of sexual orientation which results. Neither are divorced spouses, in particular men, always going to be protected in the event of family breakdown. Nor will the economically less advantaged always be able to rely on the concept of citizenship of the Union to surmount the obstacles which EC free movement law places upon them. But in each of these cases, the position would be ameliorated if the family consists entirely of EU nationals, since access to autonomous status is inherently far easier to accomplish. The fundamental distinction between EC nationals and third-country nationals still remains, despite the application of the family reunion directive, because of the extremely low standards set by that Directive. It has been accentuated by the EU's decision to give preference to its wealthy neighbours as regards free movement of persons by way of its association agreements.[34] And the stark result of that distinction is that many non-white people in the European Union cannot enjoy the human right to respect for their family life in the same way as the white majority, even if they are long-term residents of a Member State. This unethical situation, has, to its lasting shame, been endorsed by the European Court of Human Rights. It can only be hoped that greater judicial courage and political will may result in narrowing and eventual abolition of this unjustifiable distinction in the years to come.

Steve Peers is Professor of Law, University of Essex.

Footnotes

1 This paper is an adapted excerpt from Peers, 'Family Reunion and Community Law' in Walker, ed., Towards an Area of Freedom, Security and Justice (OUP, 2004).

2 Directive 2003/86 (OJ 2003 L 251/12).

3 See Hervey, 'Migrant Workers and their Families in the European Union: the Pervasive Market Ideology of Community law' in Shaw and More, eds., New Legal Dynamics of European Union (OUP, 1995) 91.

4 Art. 3(2) of Directive 2000/43 (OJ 2000 L 180/22).

5 See Abdulaziz and others v UK (Series A, no. 94), Moustaquim v Belgium (Series A, no. 193) and C v Belgium (Reports 1996-III).

6 Reports 1996-IV; see also Poirrez v France (judgment of 30 Sep. 2003, not yet reported).

7 This is a separate question from the question of whether the sponsors are the correct comparator at all when the right at issue is an autonomous right of residence for the family member (see discussion in Peers, n. 1 above).

8 For instance, see Bosphorus Airways v Ireland, judgment of the European Court of Human Rights of May 31 2005, with further references (not yet reported).

9 See Hervey (n. 3 above).

10 See Peers, s. 3.4 above.

11 See Hervey (n. 3 above); Ackers, 'Citizenship, Gender and Dependency in the European Union: Women and Internal Migration' in O'Keeffe and Hervey, eds., Sex Equality Law in the European Union (Wiley, 1995), 221; Hervey, 'A Gendered Perspective on the Right to Family Life in European Community Law' in Neuwahl and Rosas, eds., The European Union and Human Rights' (Kluwer, 1995) 221; Moebius and Szyszczak, 'Of Raising Pigs and Children' 18 YEL (1998) 125; and Ackers, 'Women, Citizenship and European Community Law: The Gender Implications of the Free Movement Provisions' 4 (1994) JSWFL 391.

12 Case C-413/99 Baumbast and R [2002] ECR I-7091; see also Case C-200/02 Chen and Zhu [2004] ECR I-9923.

13. Case C-308/93 Cabanis-Issarte [1996] ECR I-2097.

14. Case C-65/98 [2000] ECR I-4747. This case concerns a couple who were married, divorced (but still lived together) and then remarried. On the status of family members under the EC-Turkey association agreement, see Peers (n. 1 above), s. 4.

15 OJ 2004 L 16/44; see Peers, 'Implementing Equality? The Directive on

long-term resident third-country nationals', 29 ELRev. (2004) 437.

16 See cases discussed in Peers (n. 1 above), ss. 2, 3 and 4, which concerned the possible expulsion of fathers following family breakdown, divorce or divorce proceedings.

17 Ackers, 'Citizenship' (n. 11 above) at 228-237.

18 For the first argument, which is sometimes confined to arguing that the concept of family is too narrow without suggesting an ECHR breach, see Hervey (n. 3 and 11 above); Ackers, 'Women' (n. 11 above); Lundstrom, 'Family Life and the Free Movement of Workers in the European Union' 10 IJLPF (1996) 250; and Stalford, 'Concepts of Family Under EU Law – Lessons from the ECHR' 16 IJLPF (2002) 410. For the second argument, which obviously crosses over with the sex discrimination argument, but does not confine itself to the position of women, see Weiler, 'Thou Shall Not Oppress a Stranger: On the Judicial Protection of the Human Rights of Non-EC Nationals – A Critique' 3 EJIL (1992) 65. Woods ('Family Rights in the EU – Disadvantaging the Disadvantaged?' 11 (1999) CFLQ 17) covers both arguments.

19 See s. 3.4 of Peers (n. 1 above).

20 See the Opinion of 8 Sept. 2005 in Case C-540/03 *EP* v *Council*, pending, which challenged the validity of parts of the family reunion Directive in light of human rights law.

21 See Ahmut v Netherlands (Reports 1996-VI) and Gul v Switzerland (Reports 1996-I).

22 See s. 3 of Peers (n. 1 above).

23 Case C-377/98 Netherlands v EP and Council [2001] ECR I-7079 and C-36/02 Omega [2004] ECR I-9609.

24 See Lundstrom and Stralford (both n. 18 above). For an exploration of the issue before the judgments in Grant and D, see Waaldijk, 'Free Movement of Same-Sex Partners' 3 (1996) MJ 271.

25 Case 59/85 Reed [1987] ECR 1283.

26 Case C-249/96 [1998] ECR I-629 and Joined Cases C-122/99 and C-125/99 [2001] ECR I-4319.

27 Art. 3(2) of Dir. 2000/78 (OJ 2000 L 303/16).

28 See s. 3.2 of Peers (n. 1 above).

29 Stalford, 'The Citizenship Status of Children in the European Union' 8 IJCR (2000) 101.

30 On entry into vocational training and status after vocational training, see Peers (n. 1 above), ss. 3 & 4.

31 Case C-224/98 D'Hoop [2002] ECR I-6191.

32 Case C-148/02 Avello [2003] ECR I-11613).

33 Chen and Zhu (n. 12 above).

34 See s. 4 of Peers (n. 1 above), as regards the EC-Switzerland agreement on free movement of persons and the European Economic Area.

12

Switzerland votes in favour of accession to Schengen: A defeat for civil liberties

Balthasar Glattli & Heiner Busch

The issues in the referendum should have been straightforward:
● Are we in favour of closing the borders of Europe to refugees and immigrants?
● Are we in favour of a police super-computer that serves primarily as an instrument to implement this policy of exclusion?
● Are we in favour of uncontrolled information exchange between the police and security services?
● Are we in favour of giving police and border guards powers to carry out arbitrary 'non-suspect related' controls (stops and searches) inland?
● Do we want even fewer asylum seekers to have the right for their claim to be assessed in Switzerland?

These should have been the questions raised by the left with regard to the accession to Schengen and Dublin Agreements, which a majority of the Swiss population voted in favour of on 5 June. The reply by the left should have been a resounding 'No'.

Only a minority on the left posed these questions: a few Green Party members and fewer Social Democratic dissidents, the *Á Gauche Toute* coalition (the Workers' Party – PdA, *Solidarites* and Alternative Lists), a few civil liberties organisations and migrant support groups and the extra-parliamentary left.

The parliamentary left (the Social Democratic Party (SP) and the Green Party) failed to defend civil liberties in the debate on Schengen and abandoned positions it had defended for many years. Instead, it supported a yes vote for Schengen alongside the bourgeois 'centre' parties (the liberal FDP and the Christian democratic CVP), the police and their political representatives and the employers' organisations, which financed much of the Yes campaign. There are two interrelated concerns for the left's change of position: firstly, concern over the conservative-nationalist Swiss People's Party (SVP) and secondly, the EU. The SP's and the Green's Yes to Schengen is largely motivated by a strong-anti SVP reflex. The SVP had seized on the referendum to promote its racist/xenophobic policies and attempted to exploit those parts of the Swiss population who are losing out in the process of globalisation: 'Schengen – unprotected border, more illegals, more criminals, more violence, more foreigners, more unemployed Swiss people, lower wages, foreign law, EU accession.' The chain of associations made here are well known: the fairy-tale idyll of the small state with its tight and 'secure' borders which, it is claimed, will protect its inhabitants from the dangers of the outside world.

For the SP and the Greens, who have tried for years to establish themselves as pro-European parties, Schengen represented another step towards the EU. Whilst one part of the SP, led by foreign secretary Micheline Calmy-Rey and party president Hans-Jürg Fehr, went as far as selling Schengen and Dublin as a 'social-democratic project', the rest of the parliamentary left became experts in 'swallowing frogs' (i.e. accepting something that is awkward, because it is necessary). Although Schengen could not be described as a 'social democratic project', it was one that 'opened up' avenues, Hilde Fässler, head of the SP parliamentary group, announced at the end of February 2005, to the delegates' meeting of the Young Socialists.

Schengen – not an open door but a police project
Anyone taking a closer look at the history of Schengen cooperation will find it hard to comprehend the SP and Green positions. The beginnings of Schengen are to be found in the 'completion' of the Single Market, which the then European Community set as its goal at the beginning of the 1980s. The EC propagated the Single Market as an 'area without internal borders', which guaranteed the 'four freedoms': the free circulation of goods, capital, services and persons. At first, the lifting of internal border controls only played a symbolic role in this gigantic project of liberalisation and privatisation: citizens should be able to experience the borderless new Europe in a concrete way, the European Commission has said since 1985 (in its six-monthly reports on the progress made in the creation of the Single Market). After the terror hysteria of the 1970s had died down, only spot checks were carried out at internal borders. Besides, in view of increasingly dense cross-border traffic, it was impossible to implement more controls.

Nonetheless, the question of border controls became the centre of much controversy. Not only the UK and Ireland, who refused to join the project altogether, started voicing security concerns, but also the Schengen countries representing the 'Core Europe' – France,

Germany and the Benelux. Their line was: the abolition of internal border controls would create a loss of security that would have to be compensated by security measures. By the time of the Schengen Implementation Agreement (SIA) of 1990 it became apparent how imbalanced the 'free movement *vs.* compensatory measures' argument really was.

In fact, Article 2 (1) SIA lays down that everybody may cross internal borders anywhere, at any time without control. Paragraph 2 of the same Article, however, contains the disclaimer that in case of a threat against 'national security' or 'public order', controls may be 'temporarily' introduced. The Schengen states have made ample use of this exceptional clause since the Convention came into force in March 1995, not only for big football matches or anti-summit protests but also in 'normal' times. In addition to this, there are compensatory internal controls, which, although not explicitly laid down in the SIA, are carried out by all Schengen states in one form or another. In Germany, these were introduced as special police powers in the Länder police laws as well as the Federal Border Guards law under the name of *Schleierfahndung*, i.e. arbitrary stop and search operations (Hernkind, 2002, Kant 2004).

The remaining 142 Articles of the SIA concern themselves with compensatory measures:
- systematically intensifying control and surveillance at external borders,
- creating a common and necessarily more restrictive visa policy,
- banning renewed asylum applications and introducing the first country rule, whereby asylum applications could only be lodged in the first EU country the asylum seekers arrived in. This was taken over by the Dublin Convention in an almost identical form. It was already clear with the signing of the SIA that asylum politics would be determined at EU level. In 2000, the Justice and Home Affairs Council of Ministers replaced the Dublin Convention with a slightly more precise EU Regulation. The fingerprinting system Eurodac, the technical support that enabled the implementation of the first country rule, has been in place since 2003,
- intensifying cross-border police cooperation, which encompasses, firstly, comprehensive information exchange with and without a request, secondly, cross-border 'hot pursuit' and thirdly, a series of cross-border undercover methodologies (surveillance, controlled deliveries),

● creating the Schengen Information System (SIS) as the core mechanism for cooperation: since the system came online in March 1995, data on individuals with an outstanding arrest warrant has never constituted more than two percent of SIS data. Data on persons to be refused entry at borders, however, constituted between 80 and 90 percent.

Schengen cooperation developed into a true 'police laboratory'. Prior to its formal integration into EU structures by the Treaty of Amsterdam (which came into force in May 1999) the Schengen Executive Committee had passed around 170 Decisions that became part of the Schengen *acquis*. The published parts of the *acquis* amount to 473 pages in the *Official Journal of the European Community*, and often only the summary Decisions were published, not the corresponding background documents. Comprehensive documentation continues to remain unpublished (*Schengen acquis*, 2000). Also after 1999, Schengen cooperation remained firmly under the control of the executive, that is by the Justice and Home Affairs Council as well as the Commission (Holzberger/Schubert, 1998). Meanwhile, all EU Member States (UK and Ireland only partially) as well as Iceland and Norway have joined the Schengen club. The Schengen *acquis* is still the essential criterion for the accession of central and eastern European states (Leuthardt, 1999; Dietrich, 2002). It is continually extended and the EU is currently in the process of creating a second generation Schengen Information System (SIS II) as well as a Visa Information System (Statewatch, 2005).

Schengen and Switzerland

The Swiss Government (Federal Council), especially the Federal Justice and Police Department (EJPD), had shown an interest in joining Schengen since 1990. In October 1990, the then Federal Councillor for Justice and Police, the Christian Democrat Arnold Koller, established an 'Expert Commission on Border Controls' (*Expertenkommission Grenzpolizeiliche Personenkontrollen* – EGPK) led by François Leuba, a right-wing Liberal Member of the National Council (the lower chamber of the Parliament). In its intermediate report of 1991 the commission began singing the Swiss Schengen tune: without accession, it was argued, Switzerland would degenerate into an 'island of insecurity' and become the 'country of last asylum' for asylum seekers whose applications were refused in EC/EU countries

(Rechsteiner, 1991). The final report of the Leuba commission from October 1993 became a blueprint for the core elements of Switzerland's police and justice politics after the *Fichenscandal*[1]. Internally, the Expert Commission recommended 'extended state security', externally, it reiterated its commitment to Schengen. Even though there were never plans to abolish controls at Switzerland's borders, the Expert Commission adopted the Schengen rhetoric of 'loss of security' and 'compensatory measures'.

Throughout the 1990s, Switzerland maintained a peculiarly contradictory position. On the one hand, it shared the aims of the EU's Justice and Home Affairs policy, or rather, of Schengen cooperation: in the area of police and intelligence services, Switzerland adopted the threat of 'organised crime', which subsequently spawned the entire modernisation and reorganisation process that followed the *Fichenscandal*. With its policies of three (or rather two) concentric circles – excluding immigration from the outer, non-EU circle – and with the 'fight against the abuse of the asylum system', Switzerland followed the Schengen line also in matters of asylum and migration. On the other hand, the accession to Schengen failed for two reasons: firstly, because Switzerland was not a member of the EU, which for a long time was an imperative for being accepted in the illustrious club; secondly, because strict border controls – including the additional deployment of military forces in Tessin – did, at least on paper, contradict the Schengen principles, as Article 2 SIA demands the abolition of internal border controls.

Because direct Schengen accession was not possible, the Swiss Federal Department of Justice and Police (EJPD) sought convergence in three ways:

● by means of regular consultation: back in 1992, during one of his first excursions to the EC Justice and Interior Ministers' meetings, then Justice and Police chief Arnold Koller (CVP), offered his European colleagues a common automated fingerprinting system for asylum seekers (BFF, 1992). The EC ministers declined the offer, called 'Eurasyl', not because they were not interested in such a system but because they wanted to set up their own system, called Eurodac,

● by means of the independent national implementation of EU, or rather, Schengen regulations, particularly in the area of visa policy,

● by means of bilateral agreements with its neighbouring Schengen states, which would, at least partially, implement the Schengen *acquis*.

The first step in this bilateral approach was a readmission

106

agreement with Germany, signed in 1993. On the occasion of its coming into force in November 1995, the Swiss Justice and Police Department and the German federal interior ministry agreed to start talks on the creation of a 'cooperative security system' (Press Release EJPD, 27.11.95), initially covering the common borders.

In the second half of 1997, Austria took over the presidency of the Schengen Executive Committee and declared the intensification of police cooperation with Switzerland as one of the focal points of its working programme (Schengen, 1997). The first fruits of this negotiation process were seen by the end of 1997: the Swiss Justice and Police Department and Germany's and Austria's interior ministries signed 'memoranda of understanding' on cooperation at the borders (Busch, 1998). In 1998, treaties followed with France and Italy, which passed through parliament without much debate. In April 1999, federal councillor Arnold Koller was able to sign police treaties with Germany and Austria, which went much further in scope and remit than the earlier agreements (ASS, 1999). This was one of his last official acts before transferring his position in the Justice and Police Department to his party friend Ruth Metzler (CVP).

By now, Switzerland had signed readmission agreements with all neighbouring Schengen states and had negotiated common methods of police cooperation that essentially mirrored those contained in the Schengen Agreement. This included the creation of common police offices at the borders and/or fast communication channels to the police offices on the other side of the border, cross-border hot pursuit and surveillance, including the use of new surveillance technologies. The agreement with France largely repeated the Schengen wording, while the agreements with Germany and Austria considerably extended this framework: hot pursuit and surveillance remained unlimited with regard to time and space. Further, persons not suspected of having committed an offence could be put under surveillance. Cross-border undercover police actions were explicitly made legal. In particular, the regulation on granting mutual support in the case of a 'threat against public security and order' was visible during the anti-World Economic Forum protests in Davos and the anti-G8 protests in Geneva in 2003.

Furthermore, the treaty with Germany foresaw the introduction of automated information exchange between both the countries' police forces, heavily leaning on the data categories of the Schengen Information System outlined in the Implementation Agreement. In contrast to the remaining treaty regulations, these regulations were, however, not put into force, because the Justice and Police Department was already steering towards full accession to Schengen.

At the beginning of 2001, the then Department chair Metzler surprised the public with the announcement that the Federal Council intended to make accession to Schengen and Dublin the subject of the second series of bilateral negotiations with the EU. In order to achieve it, he was willing to abolish border controls between Switzerland and its neighbouring Schengen states.

By then, however, it had become obvious that this announcement would not imply the abolition of border controls *per se*. The Border Guard Corps had already argued that the abolition of static controls at the 'direct border line' would release resources that could be used for the more efficient, unpredictable, inland mobile controls (WOZ, 3.5.01). The Justice and Police Department proposed that German-style arbitrary stop and search operations (*Schleierfahndung*) were a necessary measure. A 30km 'rear border region' around the state borders was to be created and laid down in custom's law. More precise deliberations on the division of remits between the federal authorities and the cantons took place in the framework of a common project by the Depatment and the Cantons' Ministers of Police Conference, entitled USIS – Examination of the System for Internal Security (*Überprüfung des Systems der Inneren Sicherheit*). The initial plan of incorporating the Border Guard, which is part of the Federal Finance Department, in the Justice and Police Department and turning it into a 'security police reserve force of the Confederation', (or a central security police force), did not work out. The Cantons insisted on retaining their sovereignty over policing matters. However, arbitrary stop and search operations are far from being abandoned: the latest USIS report no longer contains geographical limitations but calls for arbitrary controls to be carried out on a north-south and east-west axis. The Border Guard and the Cantons' police forces are to adopt respective cooperation agreements on control operations.[2] In the wake of the Schengen referendum, representatives of the 'yes' vote said that nothing would change with regard to Switzerland's border. It was argued that because Switzerland was not part of the EU's customs union, controls of goods would stay intact, which in turn could not exist without the control of persons.

The treaties have been signed and Switzerland has taken a seat in the various 'mixed committees', where it is not allowed to vote, but where representatives of its executive can take part in negotiations. The parliament might, of course, reject legal changes brought about by a further extension of the Schengen *acquis*. But even if the 'people' did reject such legal changes by means of a referendum, the Federal Council would not consider leaving Schengen but would opt for a 'pragmatic solution'.

The self-deception of the left
It is difficult to conceive of a reason why the Swiss parliamentary left supported Schengen and Dublin and why they celebrated Switzerland's accession as a success. The parliamentary fractions of the SP and the Greens exercised considerable pressure on their members. The only SP member who dared to abstain in the final vote in the National Council, the lower chamber of Parliament, was Valerie Garbani; the only no vote from the Green party came from Geri Müller. Both fractions attempted to force their members into a left-wing yes-committee. Concerning the SP, such internal disciplinary measures could be explained by the fact that on taking office in December 2002, its own Federal Councillor, Foreign secretary Micheline Calmy-Rey, had inherited the bilateral negotiations with the EU – including the dossier of the Schengen and Dublin accession – which she had to support. The Greens however are not represented in Government and thus had no obligations of loyalty.

The categorical 'yes' to Schengen had a cost. In the referendum the issue debated was not the effect the Schengen accession would have on civil liberties, but whether Switzerland would become less or more 'secure'. The SVP retained a considerable advantage as it could not only build on the symbolic force of borders but also the dominant security discourse, which it shares with the bourgeois 'centre' parties, the CVP and FDP. The SP and Greens could not withdraw from this security debate in their fight with the SVP. They had to affirm – as Markus Notter, justice minister of the canton of Zurich, announced in the TV show *Arena* on 13 May 2005 – that border controls would not be abolished, that the Schengen Information System would create more security and that Schengen would mean a more efficient fight against child pornography, the trafficking of women or organised crime. The defence led to absurd highlights: Andreas Gross, Social Democratic member of the National Council, for example, stated at a panel discussion in Embach on 10 May that it was a 'success' that

Switzerland had been able to negotiate a special arrangement that allowed it to retain the possibility of tax evasion: 'the EU has given Switzerland a present', he declared. How much self-denial of one's own party history does it take for a Social Democrat to celebrate Switzerland's protection of tax evaders whilst the state continues to encroach on the rights of refugees?

But the Schengen debate proved even more difficult for those within the parliamentary left who not so long ago were critical or totally opposed to Schengen:

In 2002, Remo Gysin, SP member of the National Council's foreign policy commission had demanded the withdrawal of the government's negotiating mandate for Schengen accession. In a guest contribution to the weekly newspaper *WOZ* he now declared that it was a success that the originally planned 30km corridor around the borders could be averted. He did not point out, though, that as a result of Schengen arbitrary stop and search can be carried out without any boundaries (*WOZ*, 5.5.05).

Hanspeter Uster, the Green police minister in the canton of Zug, is of the opinion that 'the whole [Schengen] area will become an area of control' and that 'security is increasingly seen to occur as a result of controls and deterrence ... let us not forget: Schengen/Dublin is, after all, the product of Fortress Europe' (*Greenfo* 1/05, p.5). He justified his yes vote with the argument, that 'Fortress Switzerland' is no alternative to 'Fortress Europe'. With regard to the campaign on the Schengen vote he advised the Green party to put more emphasis on the restrictive effect Schengen would have on the right to bear firearms. However, he did not point out that the arms law under Schengen does not reach the standards proposed in the failed legislative proposals of 2002, nor did he reveal that Schengen does not prevent the Swiss army selling firearms to its retiring soldiers for 100 Swiss Franks.

The parliamentary left called on two 'crown witnesses' to support two delicate issues.

In a long-winded interview in *Le Temps* (9.4.05), the federal data protection officer and former Green Party president Hanspeter Thür whitewashed the Schengen Information System: he claimed that Schengen would improve 'transparency' as Switzerland would have to implement the EU's data protection standards and argued some Cantons would even be forced to improve existing data protection regulations. Thür should have known, however, that data protection under the Schengen Information System is heavily dependent on national regulations and therefore not legally comprehensive (Schefer, 2005). He should certainly have been aware of the fact that the existence of their legal regulations by no means guarantees implementation and that data protection in practice is far more difficult under a supranational system than in a national framework Thür did not even consider the Schengen Information System II or the Visa Information System (VIS).

The Swiss Refugee Council (SFH) absolved both parties for supporting the Dublin package. The Council repeatedly declared that the drop in asylum applications expected on accession to Dublin would relax national asylum politics – neglecting the fact that the current restrictions in asylum legislation and practice are taking place at a time that asylum application numbers are at an all-time low. The Council expects the accession to Dublin to increase the pressure on Switzerland to implement the EU's minimum standards in asylum procedures. It thereby propagates a bizarre illusion, because firstly, these minimum standards are expressly excluded from the Dublin *acquis* which Switzerland is adopting and secondly, they are indeed only minimum standards: although they recognise gender specific and non-state persecution as far as there are no 'internal flight alternatives', they also contain two serious regulations that top the miserable Swiss asylum law, namely, the possibility to deport asylum seekers after a negative first instance decision as well as a third country regulation that allows the EU to declare regions within countries plagued by civil war and repression 'safe'.

The SP and the Greens abandoned their defence of civil liberties for the expectation that Schengen/Dublin accession would bring Switzerland closer to the EU, a political aim which is a burden to both parties so long as they are unable to explain how, and with which aims and alliance partners, they want to act politically within the EU. Rather than a quasi-religious avowal of the EU, political action now should be two-fold.

Firstly, transparency is necessary with regard to how Switzerland will act in the framework of Schengen, both politically in the 'mixed committees' and also in its police activities at the borders and inland.

Secondly, the left, now more than ever, needs to initiate a debate on the EU which also deals with the latter's exclusionist policies directed against refugees and migrants and the extension of police and security surveillance.

Balthasar Glättli is political secretary of Solidarité sans frontières and co-president of the Green Party in the Canton of Zurich. Heiner Busch works for Solidarité sans frontières and the Archiv Schnüffelstaat Schweiz. He is a member of the editorial board of CILIP in Berlin and the Komitee für Grundrechte und Demokratie.

Sources

ASS *Stiftung Archiv Schnüffelstaat Schweiz* (1999) 'Über die Hintertür ins Europäische Polizeihaus. Die Verträge zwischen der Schweiz und ihren Schengener Nachbarstaaten' [Via the backdoor into the European police house. The Treaties between Switzerland and her neighbouring Schengen states], Bern, June 1999.

BFF (Federal Office for Refugees) (1992) 'Eurasyl. Machbarkeitsstudie für ein europäisches Informationssystem über Fingerabdrücke von Asylbewerbern' [Eurasylum. Feasibility study for a European information system on fingerprints of asylum seekers], Bern, June 1992.

Busch, Heiner (1995) 'Grenzenlose Polizei' [Borderless police], Münster.

Busch, Heiner (1998) 'Anschluss ans Europa der Polizeien' [Accession to the Europe of police forces] in *Bürgerrechte & Polizei/CILIP* 59 (1/1998), pp. 42-45 (followed by: documentation on the Memorandum of Understanding between Switzerland and Germany, December 1997).

Dietrich, Helmut (2002) 'Das neue Grenzregime am Bug' [The new border regime at the Bug river] in *Bürgerrechte & Polizei/CILIP* 73 (3/2001), pp. 17- 26.

Herrnkind, Martin (2002) 'Schleierfahndung – institutionalisierter Rassismus' [Arbitrary stop and stop – institutionalised racism] in *Komitee für Grundrechte und Demokratie* (ed.) 'Verpolizeilichung der Bundesrepublik Deutschland' [Germany – towards a police state], Cologne.

Holzberger, Mark & Schubert, Katina (1998) 'Schengen – Quo vadis' in *Bürgerrechte & Polizei/CILIP* 59 (1/1998), pp. 12-16.

Kant, Martina (2004) '"Evaluation" der Schleierfahndung' ['Evaluation' of arbitrary stop and search] in *Bürgerrechte & Polizei/CILIP* 77 (1/2004), pp. 46-55.

Leuthardt, Beat (1999) 'An den Rändern Europas' [On the fringes of Europe], Zürich, 1999.

Leuthardt, Beat (1994) 'Festung Europa' [Fortress Europe], Zürich, 1991.

Schefer, Markus (2005) 'Die Rechtszersplitterung schadet dem Persönlichkeitsschutz' [Legal disintegration encroaches on data protection] in *plädoyer* 2/05, pp. 30-37.

Rechsteiner, Paul (1991) 'Schnüffler aller Länder – vereinigt Euch?' [Spooks of all countries – unite?] in *Fichenfritz* 8, December 1991, p. 5.

Schengen (1997) 'Schengen – Zentrale Gruppe: Arbeitsprogramm des österreichischen Vorsitzes für das zweite Halbjahr 1997' [Schengen Central Group: Working Programme of the Austrian presidency for the second half of 1997], Brussels, 16 June 1997 – Sch/C (97) 80.

Schengen acquis (2000): Schengen-Besitzstand gemäss Artikel 1 Absatz 2 des Beschlusses 1999/435/EG des Rates v. 20. Mai 1999 [Schengen acquis according to Article 1 paragraph 2 of Council Decision 1999/435/EC of 20 May 1999], Official Journal of the European Communities, L 239, 22.9.2000.

Statewatch (2005) 'SIS II – fait accompli? Construction of EUs Big Brother database under way', London (see
http://www.statewatch.org/news/2005/may/sisII-analysis-may05.pdf).

Further material:

Solidarité sans frontiers: Dossier Schengen/Dublin
    http://www.sosf.ch/publikationen/weitere/dossier_schengen.html
    http://www.schengen.ch
WOZ-Schengen: Supplement to the weekly paper
WOZ, 22.4.2005 (edited by WOZ and *Solidarité sans frontières*)

Footnotes

1 In November 1989, a parliamentary enquiry commission published the fact that the political police had records on 900,000 persons and organisations. The commission's report was the starting point of the *Fichenskandal* (literally: record cards scandal), which did not lead to abolishing the political police (as the left had demanded), but to major reorganisations and modernisation of the country's whole police system.

2 All four USIS reports are published under www.usis.ch. The fourth report is of particular interest here, as it deals with border controls and 'national compensatory measures' (p. 57 ff.), that is arbtrary stop and stop operations and discusses four different models. The Justice and Police Department and the Cantons' Chiefs of Police Conference have agreed on the 'mix version'.

13

The denial of children's rights and liberties in the UK and the North of Ireland

Phil Scraton

'a regime of rights is one of the weaks' greatest resources.'
(Freeman 2000:279-280)

Children's rights are prescribed and protected by the United Nations Convention on the Rights of the Child (UNCRC), ratified by the UK Government in 1991. Binding in international law, the expectation is that states will develop a programme of legal and policy reform and establish formal interventionist practices compliant with the Convention's Articles. The right of children to adequate care and protection, the provision of services and facilities appropriate to their basic needs and the formulation of institutional arrangements that enable children's effective participation, particularly in decisions that impact on their lives, are central to the UNCRC and its complementary instruments.[1]

Following submission of the UK Government's initial report to the UN Committee on the Rights of the Child in 1994 the Committee raised several concerns. It criticised the lack of progress in ensuring implementation, specifically insufficiency of measures taking account of the 'best interests of the child' (Art 3.1). It noted that the low age of criminal responsibility and key aspects of national legislation concerning the administration of juvenile justice was incompatible with the Convention. Of profound concern was the ethos of guidelines for establishing and managing secure training centres and the emphasis on incarceration and punishment.

Further, that children placed in care under the social welfare system could easily be diverted to custodial centres. The Committee affirmed its commitment to the imprisonment of children as a last resort (Art 37b) and to alternatives to custody. This is best illustrated in Article 40.4, which commits member states to dealing with children in conflict with the law 'in a manner appropriate to their well-being and proportionate both to their circumstances and the offence'.

The UN Committee presented the UK Government with a raft of

recommendations giving greater priority to the general principles of the UNCRC regarding legislative and administrative measures. More specifically it recommended the raising of the age of criminal responsibility and it criticised the placement of secure training orders on 12 to 14 year-olds, indeterminate detention and the doubling of custodial sentences on 15 to 17 year-olds. It stressed the need for strategies and programmes to ensure appropriate measures promoting the physical and psychological recovery and social reintegration of children engaged by the youth justice system.

In 1999 the UK submitted its second report to the UN Committee. It followed the 1997 election of the Labour Government and was a year after the passing of the 1998 Crime and Disorder Act, which introduced a range of civil orders relating to children and overhauled the youth justice system. Using a transactional discourse of 'rights' set against 'responsibilities', and without a hint of irony, the UK Government (1999:179) stated, 'It is in the interests of children and young people themselves to recognize and accept responsibility, and to receive assistance in tackling criminal behaviour'. It commented that the UN Committee 'may have misunderstood the purpose and ethos' of secure training centres, whose 'primary purpose' was 'not penal'.

Equivocating on each of the Committee's recommendations, the UK Government defended the age of criminal responsibility set at 10 in England and Wales. It was 'appropriate ... reflecting the need to protect the welfare of the youngest'. For, in 'today's sophisticated society, it is not unjust or unreasonable to assume that a child aged 10 or older can understand the difference between serious wrong and simple naughtiness' (ibid:180). The principle being that courts could 'address offending behaviour by children ... at the earliest possible opportunity, and so nip that offending behaviour in the bud' (ibid:177). Courts would be permitted to draw inferences from the failure of an accused child to give evidence or answer questions at trial. By appearing before a criminal court children would be able 'to develop responsibility for themselves' (ibid:180). The inference was clear – the UK Government regarded the criminal courts as the site most appropriate for educating children in conflict with the law or behaving 'in an anti-social way' (ibid).

This brief and schematic overview introduces some of the issues central to the children's rights debate regarding the administration of youth justice within the UK following the ratification of the UNCRC.

The Convention provides no more than a baseline statement of children's rights and the reporting guidelines issued by the UN Committee no more than a detailed statement of minimum expectations. Yet, during the decade in which all state signatories to the Convention should have been working towards full compliance what happened in the UK amounted to a grudging acceptance of the UN Committee's concerns verging on rebuttal.

The Arrival of 'Anti-social Behaviour'
Until 1996, and the build up to the UK General Election the following year, the term 'anti-social behaviour' had appeared occasionally in popular discourse and the responses of politicians to a perceived breakdown in working class communities. The focuses of attention were 'problem families', 'lone mothers' and 'persistent young offenders'. Immediately prior to and after the Election, anti-social behaviour gained significant political currency as a 'catch-all' phrase that represented all that was ill with estates and neighbourhoods from town to city; a depiction that something was rotten at the core of the urban heartland. The background to and significance of these political developments, their media representation and policy consequences have been detailed elsewhere (see: Scraton 1997; Haydon and Scraton 2000; Scraton 2002a; Scraton and Haydon 2002; Scraton 2004). Within a year of being in office the Labour Government introduced the 1998 Crime and Disorder Act which made anti-social behaviour subject to a civil injunction: the Anti-Social Behaviour Order (ASBO). By the time further legislation, the 2003 Anti-social Behaviour Act, was introduced anti-social behaviour had become established as a central plank in the Labour Administration's political programme. Yet, in definition and in context anti-social behaviour remained conceptually ambiguous resulting in inconsistent, and occasionally bizarre, interpretations and applications in the courts.

Within a relatively short period ASBOs have developed from being used against children only in exceptional circumstances to a situation in which the majority are targeted against children and young people. Based on primary research and drawing on previously published work (Scraton 2004), this paper traces these developments in the UK. It then moves on to consider the implications of the extension of the legislation to Northern Ireland (Anti-Social Behaviour [Northern Ireland] Order 2004). It argues that the failure to consider the particular circumstances and complexities of context within which anti-social behaviour is defined and regulated is markedly significant in the North of Ireland where punishment beatings and exiling already prevail in many communities.

'Tough on Crime ...'

> *'By the mid 1990s crime was rising, there was escalating family breakdown, drug abuse, and social inequalities had widened. Many neighbourhoods had become marked by vandalism, violent crime and the loss of civility. The basic recognition of the mutuality of duty and reciprocity of respect on which civil society depends appeared lost ... the moral fabric of community was unravelling.'* (Blair 2002:26)

As the British Prime Minister formally introduced the 2002 Queen's Speech outlining the Government's annual agenda, his language was familiar: 'crime and social breakdown'; diminished 'quality of life'; 'social disintegration', and so on. The 'new opportunities' in health, welfare and education claimed by Blair could not be experienced 'if people walk out of their doors and are confronted by abuse, vandalism, and anti-social behaviour'. A 'new, simpler and tougher approach to anti-social behaviour' would be the priority. He continued, 'It is petty crime and public nuisance that causes so much distress ... vandalism, graffiti, low-level aggression and violence ... Families have a right to be housed. But they have no right to terrorise those around them'. As the 'war on terror' was being mobilised globally so the war on terror at home would be pursued relentlessly. In Blair's analysis the issues are primarily moral and social rather than political and structural (see: Scraton 2002b).

Blair's explanation for the upsurge in petty crime, anti-social behaviour and public nuisance was predictable but more in keeping with successive Home Secretaries' utterances throughout the Conservative Thatcher and Major years. He attacked the criminal justice system as outmoded, over-indulging offenders. Courts were slow in processing cases and out of touch with the needs and demands of justice administered in the 21st Century. Welfare approaches continued to dominate proceedings, bending to accommodate defendants in their pleas of mitigation and in lenient sentences. In this skewed process consideration for perpetrators had become prioritised above the needs of victims. Hard core, persistent offenders, presented by Blair as responsible for the majority of crimes committed, were tolerated, even excused. In high risk neighbourhoods police were thin on the ground, overburdened with peripheral duties. Thus, un-policed low level crime and anti-social behaviour had escalated. Despite the emphasis in recent legislation on multi-agency strategies, inter-agency initiatives were neither efficient nor effective. For those prosecuted, the public perception, assumed by Blair as reality, was that the punishments meted out failed to reflect the seriousness of the offences committed. Only by remedying such issues and imbalances, by addressing low-level crime and by broadening the definitional scope of anti-social behaviour, would 'social cohesion' be restored to 'fragmented communities' (ibid). Blair's message was not new.

A decade earlier, as Shadow Home Secretary, Blair deplored the 'moral vacuum' prevalent throughout British society. Instructing children and their disaffected communities in 'the value of what is right and what is wrong', offered the only salvation from the sure descent into 'moral chaos'. A future Labour government, he promised, would be 'tough on crime and tough on the causes of crime' (*The Guardian*, 20 February 1993). He was speaking in the immediate aftermath of the abduction and killing of 2-year-old James Bulger by two 10-year-olds, Jon Venables and Robert Thompson. Taking an exceptional situation, however serious, out of its specific context displayed political opportunism rather than analytical awareness. Those events, he continued, were 'hammer blows against the sleeping conscience of the nation'. The distasteful metaphor was not lost in a media caught up in the 'crime of the decade'.

The killing of James Bulger occurred within the context of 'a fermenting body of opinion that juvenile justice in particular, and penal liberalism in general, had gone too far' (Goldson 1997:129). During the early 1990s a series of unrelated disturbances in towns throughout England and Wales raised the profile of youth offending. Media coverage focused on 'joyriding', 'ram-raiding', 'bail bandits' and 'persistent young offenders'. Senior police officers directed sustained pressure at Government to address the 'issue' of repeat offending. The elevation of James Bulger's tragic death as the ultimate expression of a 'crisis' in childhood offered an unprecedented opportunity for leading politicians to out-tough each other. It was exploited to the full, 'a catalyst for the consolidation of an authoritarian shift in youth justice ... a shift which, in legal and policy initiatives, was replicated throughout all institutional responses to children and young people' (Scraton 1997:170).

118

Phil Scraton

... Tough on Liberties

> '*Property owners, residents, retailers, manufacturers, town planners, school authorities, transport managers, employers, parents and individual citizens – all of these must be made to recognize that they to have a responsibility [for preventing and controlling crime], and must be persuaded to change their practices in order to reduce criminal opportunities and increase informal controls.*' (Garland 1996:445)

However clumsy, the term 'responsibilisation' carries a simple message: the state alone cannot, nor should it be expected to, deliver safe communities in which levels of crime and fear of crime are significantly reduced and potential victims are afforded protection. While private organisations, public services and property owners take measures to tackle opportunistic crime, thus turning the private security provision into one of the most lucrative contemporary service industries, in addressing prevention the 'buck stops' with parents and individual citizens. Civil rights, including rights of access to state support, intervention and benefits, are presented as the flip-side of civic responsibilities. Being responsible for challenging intimidatory behaviour, small-scale disorder and criminal activity is part of a network of 'informal controls' contributing towards safer and more cohesive communities. At the hub of this idealised notion of 'community' is the relationship between families and inter-agency partnerships working towards common, agreed social objectives. The live connection between a new form of communitarianism and the liberal tradition of shared responsibility underpinned the much-vaunted 'Third Way' politics adopted by Clinton's Democrats and Blair's 'New' Labour.

New Labour's reclamation of 'community' was consistently evident in Blair's remoralisation thesis that first surfaced in the aftermath of James Bulger's tragic death. Five years on he stated: 'Community defines the relationship not only between us as individuals, but also between people and the society in which they live, one that is based on responsibilities as well as entitlements' (quoted in Gould 1998:234). For Blair, rewards to individuals are earned through altruism, whether meeting family obligations or community responsibilities. Core values and principles are derived, therefore, in the mutually beneficial and benevolent social transactions between the 'self' and others; 'others' being the mirror in which self-respect is reflected, an image made tangible through 'communitarianism'.

Within this process of reclamation, itself a form of moral renewal, crime represents a betrayal of the self and a betrayal of the immediate social relations of family and community. The corrective for crime, however petty, and for disruptive or disorderly behaviours, is two-dimensional. First, affirming culpability and responsibility through the due (and assumed to be fair) process of criminal justice – from apprehension to punishment incorporating the expectations of retribution and remorse. Second, the reconstruction of and support for the proven values of positive families and strong communities. The New Labour agenda established the priority of crime prevention within all public agencies. The social objective was early intervention – targeting children's potentially criminal behaviour in a context of 'appropriate' parenting. It extended to a promised increase in secure accommodation for young offenders and 'curfews for 10-year-olds' (*Sunday Times* 18 August 1996).

Following the 1997 Labour victory, Home Secretary Jack Straw returned the popular debate to familiar territory: 'Today's young offenders can too easily become tomorrow's hardened criminals' supported by 'an excuse culture [that] has developed within the youth justice system' (*The Guardian*, 28 November 1997). It was an inefficient youth justice system that 'often excuses young offenders who come before it, allowing them to go on wasting their own and wrecking other people's lives'. Meanwhile parents 'are not confronted with their responsibilities' and 'offenders are rarely asked to account for themselves' (ibid). Straw's message was unambiguous: victims were disregarded, the public was excluded.

He reiterated four key propositions. First, when tolerated or indulged, the disruptive and offensive behaviour of children leads inevitably to their eventual participation in serious and repetitive crimes. Second, that within the community, the primary responsibility for regulating and policing such behaviour rests with parents. Third, professionals entrusted on 'society's behalf' with initiating purposeful, correctional interventions had betrayed that trust, excusing unacceptable levels of behaviour and their own lack of effectiveness. Fourth, existing processes and procedures over-represent the needs and rights of perpetrators while under-representing victims.

From within the prevailing political rhetoric, endorsed by the independent Audit Commission (1996), emerged the ubiquitous and conveniently elastic term 'anti-social behaviour'. Its new-found status quickly consolidated as the key issue. As journalists, academics and practitioners sought a more precise definition the newly elected Government obliged with a less than precise definition via a rushed consultation document. It was defined as behaviour that 'causes harassment to a community; amounts to anti-social criminal conduct, or is otherwise anti-social; disrupts the peaceful and quiet enjoyment of a neighbourhood by others; intimidates a community or section of it' (Local Government Information Unit, 1997). The slide between 'criminal conduct' and 'anti-social behaviour' was calculated and reflected in the ambiguity of 'otherwise' amounting to a definition open to broad interpretation and subject to conveniently wide discretion in its enforcement. A group of established academics, one of whom – Rod Morgan – later was appointed as the Head of the Youth Justice Board, collectively attacked the conceptualisation of anti-social behaviour as, 'neither sensible nor carefully targeted' (Ashworth et al 1998:7). They condemned the proposed legislation for taking 'sweepingly defined conduct within its ambit', granting 'local agencies virtually unlimited discretion to seek highly restrictive orders', jettisoning 'fundamental legal protections for the granting of these orders', while authorising 'potentially draconian and wholly disproportionate penalties for violations' (ibid). Rather than providing effective interventions to tackle 'those who terrorise their neighbours', the 'actual reach is far broader', covering 'a wide spectrum of conduct deemed anti-social, whether criminal or not'. The early warnings, exposing the implicit authoritarianism within the Bill, went unheeded. The consultation period was brief and failed to develop an inclusive practitioner-informed debate. Politically, it is fair to assume, that was the intention.

Consequently the 1998 Crime and Disorder Act (CDA) quietly became law, its wide-ranging content introduced over three years. Generically it aimed to reduce crime, improve community safety, promote more effective multi-agency approaches and increase public confidence in the criminal justice system. To these ends it obliged local authorities to present a crime strategy derived in a crime and disorder audit involving consultation with local communities, 'hard to reach' groups and all public sector agencies. It placed a responsibility on statutory agencies to participate in the operational planning, realisation and evaluation of local strategies.

In addition to the overhaul of youth justice, the CDA abolished the presumption of *doli incapax* (incapable of crime) and allowed courts to draw inferences from the failure of an accused child to give evidence or refusal to answer questions at trial. Parenting Orders, Child Safety Orders and local Child Curfew Schemes were also significant new developments. Perhaps the most immediately contentious initiative, however, was the introduction of Anti-Social Behaviour Orders (ASBOs). These community-based civil injunctions, applied for by the police or the local authority – each in consultation with the other – were to be taken against an individual or a group of individuals (eg families) whose behaviour was considered 'anti-social'. Applications were to be made to the magistrates' court, acting in its adult jurisdiction and in its civil function, with provision for the use of professional witnesses. ASBOs were considered, in principle, to be preventative measures targeting 'persistent and serious' anti-social behaviour. Anti-social behaviour was defined as 'acting in a manner that caused or is likely to cause distress to one or more persons not in the same household as himself [sic]'. The 1998 Act Guidelines stated that 'prohibitions in the order must be such as are necessary to protect people from further anti-social acts by the defendant in the locality', targeting 'criminal or sub-criminal behaviour, or minor disputes ...' (CDA Introductory Guide, Section 1). A criminal offence was committed only on breach of the order without a 'reasonable excuse'.

Instructively, given the pattern of events that followed, the Guidelines stated that ASBOs would 'be used mainly against adults' (ibid). This commitment was affirmed by the UK Government's (1999) submission to the UN Committee on the Rights of the Child in which it set out the changes in legislation regarding children. While all other CDA orders were discussed, the ASBO was omitted suggesting that it was of little, if any, significance regarding the behaviour of children. Given that the Crime and Disorder Act concentrated heavily on the criminal and disorderly behaviour of 10 to 18 year olds, and was the vehicle through which youth justice was structurally reconfigured, it is unsurprising that it came to be viewed as legislation primarily concerned with the regulation and criminalisation of children and young people. The UK Government's submission to the UN Committee states that 'it is not unjust or unreasonable to assume that a child aged 10 or older can understand the difference between serious wrong and simple naughtiness'. But, it proposed, for children lacking 'this most basic moral understanding, it is all the more imperative that appropriate intervention and rehabilitation should begin as soon as possible' (ibid:180).

'Serious wrong' and 'simple naughtiness' were presented as

opposite ends of a spectrum, yet no acknowledgement was made regarding the complexities of understanding, experience and interpretation that lie between. Also significant are issues of premeditation, intent and spontaneity. As stated elsewhere, '[r]educing these complexities, difficult to disentangle at any age, to simple opposites in the minds of young children amounts to incredible naivety or purposeful misrepresentation' (Haydon and Scraton 2000:429). Further, the courts are proposed as 'the site most appropriate to intervene and rehabilitate ...' (ibid). Yet, the UK Government (1999:180) stated that 'emphasis is firmly placed not on criminalizing children, but on helping them to recognise and accept responsibility for their actions and enabling them to receive help to change their offending behaviour'.

The combination of major institutional change in youth justice, new civil injunctions – particularly ASBOs, the removal of *doli incapax* and the right to silence and an expansion in secure units sealed the Labour Government's intent to 'out-tough' its predecessors. As Johnston and Bottomley (1998:177) state, while 'the Conservatives talked tough, it is Labour that introduced stringent measures such as child curfews, anti-social behaviour orders and parenting orders'. The result was a 'regulatory-disciplinary approach to crime prevention, combined with welfarist assistance to help people meet its standards'. What the Crime and Disorder Act exemplifies is the tangible outcome of New Labour's law and order rhetoric; 'an amalgam of "get tough" authoritarian measures with elements of paternalism, pragmatism, communitarianism, responsibilization and remoralization' (Muncie 1999:169). It was to be delivered, using the language and theory of 'risk', through a 'burgeoning new managerialism whose new depth and legal powers might best be described as "coercive corporatism"' (ibid).

Writing as the Act was being implemented, Allen (1999:22) registered concern regarding the net-widening potential of targeting anti-social behaviour alongside the increasingly 'coercive approach of zero-tolerance policing' interventions leading to the promotion rather than eradication of 'social exclusion'. Thus the 'promise of speedier trials, new teams and panels to monitor action plans, restorative justice and the inadequacies of the pre-1998 system' was the justification for the Crime and Disorder Act but the fast-emerging concerns voiced by academics and practitioners included 'its potential for net-widening, over control, lack of safeguards and what one can only call 'joined-uplabelling' (Downes 2001:9). Goldson (2000:52) put this position more strongly: 'Early intervention, the erosion of legal safeguards and concomitant criminalisation, is packaged as a courtesy to the child'. Yet it amounted to 'an interventionism which "promotes prosecution" ... violates rights and, in the final analysis will serve only to criminalise the most structurally vulnerable children' (ibid).

Introduced without any convincing evidence of the 'graduation' of 'at risk' children and young people into crime, ASBOs received 'a degree of political backing out of all proportion to their potential to reduce crime and disorder' while the 'demonisation' of parents through Parenting Orders 'will exacerbate a situation' that was 'already complex and strained' (Hester 2000:166/171). Hester predicted that ASBOs would be used primarily in 'poor communities' and 'by definition' would be 'disproportionately deployed' (ibid:172). More problematic still, the policing and regulation of children and parents within the most politically and economically marginal neighbourhoods effectively expects people to take responsibility for all aspects of their lives in social and material contexts where they are least able to cope. As Pitts (2001:140) reflected, the 'managerial annexation of youth justice social work ... effectively transformed [social workers] into agents of the legal system, preoccupied with questions of "risk", "evidence" and "proof", rather than "motivation", "need" and "suffering". In interpreting the Labour Government's swift delivery of the Crime and Disorder Act and its concentration on ASBOs Gardner et al (1998:25) noted the contradiction in 'tackling social exclusion' while passing legislation 'destined to create a whole new breed of outcasts'.

Within a year the Government strongly criticised local authorities for failing to implement child curfews and ASBOs, thus intensifying pressure on local authorities to establish anti-social behaviour initiatives. Newly appointed or seconded staff, often under-trained and poorly managed, were impelled into using ASBOs without having the time or opportunity to plan appropriately for their administration or consequences. ASBOs soon became a classic example of net-widening through which children and young people in particular, who previously would have been cautioned, became elevated to the first rung of criminalisation's ladder. The vindictiveness of local media, alongside the triumphalism of local councillors and their officers, provide dramatic illustrations of the public humiliation associated with authoritarian policies conveyed through sensationalist reporting.

Naming and shaming

Liverpool's first ASBO was served on a disruptive 13-year-old. On 5 June 2002 the *Liverpool Echo* dedicated its entire front page to the case. A large photograph of the child's face was placed alongside a banner headline: 'THUG AT 13'. Within a month he was sentenced to eight months for his third breach of the ASBO. Also in June 2002 the *Wigan Reporter* gave its front page to a 'mini menace' who was to be 'sent on a trip to a remote Scottish island' where 'there was nothing to break and nothing to steal'. The headline read 'COUNCIL FUND SCOTTISH TRIP FOR A TINY TERROR'. The caption under the colour photograph named the 13 year old, stating: 'The youngster leaves court, pretending to play the flute with his screwed-up anti-social court order'. A case in West Lancashire, involving the banning of a brother and sister from a specified neighbourhood, was headlined 'STAY OUT!' and 'Taming two tearaways' (*Skelmersdale Advertiser* 30 May 2002). Such cases were not exceptions. Children, not charged with any criminal offence, were named and shamed and their neighbours were invited to note the conditions attached to ASBOs and report any breach to the authorities.

On 20 March 2002 *The Mirror*, proclaiming on its masthead the award of 'newspaper of the year', devoted the full front page to the photographs of two boys, aged 15 and 17. Above their faces ran the heading: 'REVEALED: The lawless teenagers who are laughing at us all. Every town has them'. Beneath the photographs, occupying a quarter of the page was the word 'VILE'. Under each photograph were boxes arrowed to the faces above: 'Ben, age 17 Crimes: 97'; 'Robert, age 15 Crimes: 98'. The distinction between 'crime' and 'anti-social behaviour' was not made and the two page detailed coverage would not have been permitted had they been convicted of crimes.

In September 2003 ASBOs were obtained against seven young men. One was issued for life, a second for 10 years and the remainder for five years. The hearing lasted for 15 weeks and there followed a five week hearing in the crown court which dismissed their appeal application. 3,000 copies of a police approved leaflet entitled 'KEEPING CRIME OFF THE STREETS OF BRENT' were distributed, containing photographs of the seven young men, their names, their ages and the details of the orders. The local authority posted details of the proceedings on its website, describing the gang as 'animalistic', 'thugs' and 'bully-boys'. It justified the publicity by stating the necessity to keep people in the community fully informed. The behaviour of the seven young men had been threatening, abusive and violent to the extent that many residents were fearful in their homes. The use of leaflets, the website and the community newsletter was considered an exceptional response to an exceptional case. Yet it had set a precedent in issuing photographs and personal details, demonstrating a commitment to using publicity as part of the ASBO enforcement strategy.

On 17 February 2004 the *Daily Express* devoted its front page to the headline: 'TERRORISED BY GIRL GANG BOSS AGED 13: She led 50 hooligans on violent rampage'. Alongside the story, particularly significant because of her age and gender, was her photograph and name. Under the Page 9 headline, 'High on glue, the teen gang leader who spread alarm and fear to a city', were the 12 conditions of her five year ASBO. Among these were: mixing with 42 named young people, 'the Leeds Town Crew'; using the terms 'Leeds Town Crew', 'LTC', 'TWOC Crew', 'GPT', 'Cash Money Boyz', or 'CMB', in any correspondence, spoken or written; barred from areas of central Leeds unless accompanied by parent, guardian, social or youth worker; travelling on buses unless accompanied by parent or guardian; wearing a hood or scarf that might obscure her identity. As she left the court she pulled up her hood to guard against the press photographers and instantly breached her ASBO.

The *News of the World* (10 October 2004) exposed a young child and his family to serious risks of reprisals. Across two inside pages it ran the 'Exclusive': 'Stefan is first 11-year-old to have Anti-Social Behaviour Order served on him'. A full page showed the child behind a driving wheel, the headline took up half a page: 'YOUNGEST THUG IN BRITAIN!' Alongside a 'stamp' marked 'OFFICIAL', it listed the 'Tiny tearaway's rap sheet from hell'. The list included: 'Theft'; 'Drugs'; 'Booze'; 'Arson'; Joy-riding'; 'Truancy'. It concluded: 'TOTAL NIGHTS LOCKED UP IN JAIL: 50'. On the opposite page was a photograph of Stefan seated with his mother and father and seven brothers and sisters. Under the heading 'Crowded house', Stefan's face and those of his parents were visible. The faces of the other children were pixillated to 'protect their identities'. The headline was condemnatory: 'Yob's jobless parents rake in equivalent of more than £40k a year'. The story-line was unforgiving: 'He's 11 years old – and terrifying. A swaggering little shoplifting, fire-raising, joyriding, fighting, drinking, drug-taking, nightmare doted on by his benefit-sponging parents'.

The child protection issues in the presentation of this story are self-evident but the *News of the World* was fortified by the fact that earlier in the week 'three yobs failed in a High Court bid to prove that publicity about their ASBOs had infringed their human rights'. This was a reference to the 'right to privacy challenge' brought by three claimants supported by the civil liberties' group, Liberty, against the Metropolitan Police Commissioner, the London Borough of Brent and the Home secretary over the 'Keep Crime off the Streets of Brent' leaflet referred to above. The claimants alleged that the extent of the publicity was unlawful, breaching Article 8 of the European Convention on Human Rights. They argued that the publicity was disproportionate and unnecessary particularly in its reference to personal details couched in sensational language. Responding that the content of the publicity was already in the public domain, the police submitted that public confidence had to be restored, ASBOs required local support in their enforcement and publicity was an essential factor in securing deterrence.

The Court held that where 'publicity was intended to inform, reassure, assist in enforcing the orders and deter others, it would not be effective unless it included photographs, names and partial addresses'. Local residents had experienced 'significant criminal behaviour' over an extended period, the individuals concerned were well known in the area and the publicity was central to ending their anti-social activities. The publicity's 'colourful language' was necessary to draw residents' attention to the issue. The Judge criticised the claimants' protracted legal challenges, stating that time limits should be imposed on contesting ASBOs. The claimants 'had been shown to be members of a gang responsible for serious anti-social behaviour over an extended period' and had been 'stopped, searched arrested and brought before the courts' yet they had 'continued with anti-social behaviour and defiance of authority' (quoted in *The Guardian*, 8 October 2004). In this context the publicity and language was considered appropriate.

The Leader of Brent Council expressed surprise that Liberty had supported the case given the claimants' 'serious and persistent bad behaviour', which had been 'dangerous, threatening and violent'. The judgment, she stated, had been awaited with interest by local authorities throughout England and Wales. A Home Office spokesperson considered that it supported the Home Secretary's policies and determination to tackle anti-social behaviour. The principle, that 'publicity is necessary to help with the enforcement of an order', had been established by the court. It was clear that the judges took the view that the criminal and anti-social behaviour of the extended gang had been so serious and sustained that their identities were already well known, their reputations well established. By their actions they had compromised their right to privacy.

'Crusading against crime': a brief case study[2]
Newtown is a Northern second generation new town built in the 1970s within a shire county. Of the eight districts within the county it has the lowest recorded crime rate yet from the outset showed a marked enthusiasm for the clampdown on antisocial behaviour and was quick to establish and anti-social behaviour team. The anti-social behaviour co-ordinators stated their reluctance to be over-eager in seeking ASBOs, maintaining they should be used as a last resort and then only in extreme cases and with appropriate and workable arrangements for their administration in place. Yet the political dynamics were considerable:

> *'There was massive pressure on us. We needed an ASBO. The [area] hadn't had one and the Chief Executive was on the case all the time. The police hadn't had one, the Council hadn't had one, so we had to get one.'* (Personal interview)

The investment in and success of the anti-social behaviour unit was tied to:

> *'... how many evictions I get and how many anti-social behaviour orders, injunctions and how many notices seeking possessions I serve. It always gets in the paper and I know that's how my bosses think I'm doing my job well ... the more evictions and anti-social behaviour orders I get, the better I'm doing.'* (Personal interview)

Naming and shaming played a significant part in Newtown's determination to 'get tough' on anti-social behaviour. The local newspaper ran the front page headline 'FIRST YOBBO TO BE BARRED: Tough new line to stop louts terrorising neighbourhoods'. It published two photographs and stated that the 10 conditions imposed on the 18 year old, 'James', ended the 'yob's reign of terror'.

Interviews with James and his mother, Mary, provide stark testimonies regarding the impact of restrictions and media coverage. James had caused considerable disruption within his neighbourhood for several years. Of 'mixed-race' parents James endured racism on a daily basis in a predominantly white community. This came to a head when he brought home a present for his step-father. James' mother recalls:

> *'James said, "Dad, Look what I've bought yer" and Billy (step-father) turned round and said "You're not mine. I've only got one son. You're a nigger." And I think it all went downhill from there.'* (Lawrenson 2002:29)

James and Mary were convinced that racism played a significant part in being singled out for an ASBO. He was an easily recognisable target from a group of twelve boys who hung around the shops each night. Once the ASBO had been served and multiple copies of his newspaper photograph appeared across the windows of Newtown's superstore, his notoriety was complete.

> *'If I stand anywhere longer than 10 minutes I can get arrested! It upsets me mum. They put it in the papers and that, said it wasn't even gonna be front page or anything like that, and then it was all over the front page! Done me head in, man.'* (ibid:31)

Neither his solicitor nor the magistrates who heard the case were aware that reporting restrictions on the case did not apply. With the entire community aware of his 'Yobbo' status James was on the receiving end of a barrage of racist, verbal abuse whenever he went any where in the community. A woman 'started giving me loads (shouting at him). I hadn't done anything ... saying, "Ah, you can't say anything to me", and stuff like that. It's mad.' Mary stated:

> *'Young lads shouted at him: "Ah, you've got an ASBO, you can't touch me, you fat bastard" and all that stuff. He's had everything. It's like they're taunting him to have a go.'*

James was critical of his treatment by the police on the street where, 'they think they're kings, walking with their heads held high, lookin' at you like you're dirt ... they're lovin it' (ibid:47).

Banned for 8 months from entering his home James' mother was aware that the house was under surveillance.

> *'It's been horrible. I feel like I'm livin' in a godfish bowl. Permanently watched and judged. Scared of every movement me or the kids make. God knows how James must feel. One time it was throwin' it down (heavy rain). James is outside, soakin' wet, freezin' and cryin' and I'm inside cryin'. Helpless. There's nothing I could do.'* (ibid:32)

James was in no doubt about the family's neighbours and their intention to have the family evicted: 'They're all grasses ... like people goin' to the Council an' that over me mum about me bein' in the house ... it's a sad life ... nothin' better to do than chuck me mum out with twin babies, out on the streets'. The consequences were dire.

> *'They (local authority) took me to court sayin' I'd let James in the house. They said at first it was neighbours who'd seen him, then they changed it and said it was council workers (ASBO Unit). But then said a warden had seen him, "leanin' against the property, changing his socks and drying his hair, but it had been raining heavily". So he wasn't in the property! I'd probably give him some dry socks and a towel if it was raining!'*

The case was dismissed as the witnesses failed to appear before the court. Within a year James was given a custodial sentence for breaching his ASBO. This resulted in an open letter from the Chief Executive, 'on behalf of all law-abiding citizens', thanking the local newspaper 'for again giving front-page coverage to the crusade against crime'. The 'jailing' had 'remove[d] from the streets an individual who appears to be hell-bent on causing mayhem and who appears to show no remorse'. Also, 'particularly because of the high profile coverage and the fact that the [newspaper's] editorial line has not minced words on this issue – we have sent out a message loud and clear to '[Name] Wannabies' that the community will not stand idly by watching their thuggery go unchecked'.

Carry on regardless ...
As the academic debate regarding 'responsibilisation' and 'communitarianism' continued, it became clear that in the public domain the 'responsible community' was mobilised as a blunt instrument to regulate, marginalise and punish children whose behaviour was labelled in some way anti-social. Far from selective and exceptional use, the popular and much publicised assumption that ASBOs apply primarily to the behaviour of children and young people has consolidated.

While local authorities have been inconsistent in their implementation of the new legislation, new interventionist initiatives continued to develop. The Government's Social Exclusion Unit, through its National Strategy for Neighbourhood Renewal, prioritised target-setting for measurable reductions in anti-social behaviour. Central to this process was the adoption, by the Youth Justice Board, of a Risk Factors Screening Tool as 'suggested by research' (YJB/CYPU, 2002:15-16). To assess, track and monitor children and young people 0 to 16 years, 29 risk factors were specified including: holding negative beliefs and attitude (supportive of crime and other anti-social acts – not supportive of education and work); involved in offending or anti-social behaviour at a young age; family members involved in offending; poor family relationships; friends involved in anti-social behaviour; hangs about with others involved in anti-social behaviour; underachievement at school; nonattendance or lack of attachment to school. Lack of participation in structured, supervised activities and 'lack of concentration' were further indicators.

National policies for tackling anti-social behaviour were presented as coherent and comprehensive, protecting those 'at risk', processing effectively a 'hard core' of repeat offenders and challenging 'deep-seated' problems within the most vulnerable and 'deprived' areas. Yet, as far as children and young people are concerned, the indications have been that anti-social behaviour units, and those recruited to them, are engaged in a targeting process which selectively employs a range of risk factors, each open to interpretation. These were broad discretionary powers implemented by teams more informed by an ideology of policing than one of support. For example, the opening sentence of Liverpool Anti-Social Behaviour Unit's draft strategy for 2003-2006 stated that the Unit enjoyed 'notable success as a reactive punitive service' (Liverpool ASBU 2003:1).

Despite concerns being raised regarding the administration, use and consequences of the 'first wave' of ASBOs the Home Office launched new guidance in November 2002, extending and strengthening powers through the 2002 Police Reform Act. These included: the issuing of interim ASBOs; the widening of their geographical scope up to and including England and Wales; the extension of orders against people convicted of a criminal offence. In April 2003 Acceptable Behaviour Contracts (ABCs) were introduced. These are voluntary agreements through which those 'involved in' anti-social behaviour commit to acceptable behaviour. In November 2002 the then Home Secretary, David Blunkett, announced the appointment of the Director of the newly established Home Office Anti-Social Behaviour Unit, intended as a 'centre of excellence on anti-social behaviour, with experts from across Government and local agencies' (Home Office Press Release, 14 November 2002).

In March 2003 the White Paper, Respect and Responsibility –

Taking a Stand Against Anti-Social Behaviour, was published. David Blunkett introduced the document with a challenge to parents, neighbours and local communities to take: 'a stand against what is unacceptable ... vandalism, litter and yobbish behaviour' (Home Office, 2003: Foreword). He continued: 'We have seen the way communities spiral downwards once windows are broken and not fixed, streets get grimier and dirtier, youths hang around street corners intimidating the elderly/ crime goes up and people feel trapped' (ibid). The agenda included: more police officers, the consolidation of community support officers, neighbourhood warden schemes, crime and disorder partnerships, increased use of ASBOs, fixed penalty notices for disorder offences and new street crime initiatives.

The White Paper also focused on families, children and young people with particular reference to the prevention of anti-social behaviour. Its premise was that 'healthy communities are built on strong families' in which parents 'set limits' and 'ensure their children understand the difference between right and wrong' (ibid:21). On the justification that children and young people were 'at risk', a 'new Identification, Referral and Tracking system (IRT)' was to be universally adopted 'to enable all agencies to share information' (ibid:22). Information on antisocial behaviour given to the police would be 'shared with schools, social services, the youth service and other agencies ...'

Families 'described as "dysfunctional"' or 'chaotic' would be targeted. Parenting classes were regarded as 'critical in supporting parents to feel confident in establishing and maintaining a sense of responsibility, decency and respect in their children, and in helping parents manage them' (ibid:23). The White Paper quoted the Youth Justice Board's evaluation that Parenting Orders issued under the 1998 Crime and Disorder Act 'contributed to a 50% reduction in reconviction rates in children whose parents take up classes' (ibid:25). Parenting Orders would be extended giving schools and local education authorities powers to initiate parenting contracts. Refusal by parents to sign contracts would constitute a criminal offence. Intensive fostering would be imposed on families unwilling or unable to provide support.

Youth Offender Teams were also to be given powers to initiate Parenting Orders 'related to anti-social or criminal type behaviour in the community where the parent is not taking active steps to prevent the child's behaviour ...' (ibid:34). The issuing of children under 16 with ASBOs would oblige courts to serve a concurrent Parenting Order. Based on 2001 figures, which number persistent young offenders in England and Wales at 23,393, Intensive Supervision and Surveillance Programmes (ISSPs) would be initiated, 'combin(ing) community based surveillance with a comprehensive and sustained focus on tackling the factors that contribute to a person's offending behaviour' (ibid). Individual Support Orders will be used to ensure that children aged 10 to 17, against whom more than half all ASBOs are issued, address their anti-social behaviour.

Fixed Penalty Notices (FPNs) were to be administered by police officers, school and local education authority staff to parents who 'condone' or 'ignore' truancy. Notices might also be issued to parents of children 'where the children's behaviour would have warranted action ... were they to be 16 or over' (ibid : 9). The White Paper stated that sanctions directed towards children and families 'involved in anti-social activity' were 'strong' but the 'principle' remained 'consistent' – 'the protection of the local community must come first' (ibid : 35). This brief excursion into the White Paper's proposals demonstrates that harsh measures and unprecedented discretionary powers became central to essentially authoritarian cross-agency interventions.

In October 2003 the Government gave the results of a Home Office survey which recorded 66,000 anti-social behaviour incidents at an estimated daily cost of £13.4 million. The Prime Minister stated that powers should be used 'not occasionally, not as a last resort' but 'with real energy'. And should the extended powers of the imminent 2004 legislation prove insufficient 'we will go further and get you them' (*The Guardian* 15 October 2003). Yet the potential for applying ASBOs with 'real energy' had not been lost on judges. In February 2003 a Manchester district judge lifted reporting restrictions on a 17-year-old and, in addition to serving an 18 months detention order, imposed an ASBO. Breach of the ASBO carried a further period in detention of up to 5 years. Eight months later, also in Manchester, another 17-year-old was served with a 10 year ASBO in addition to an 18 months detention and training order. In this case the ASBO was sought after sentencing and while the young person was detained in custody. The terms of the ASBO were not restricted to his home area but extended throughout England and Wales. Used alongside sentencing ASBOs had become a form of 'release under licence'.

While Manchester City Council led the way in the use and expansion of the terms of ASBOs the picture across the UK remained inconsistent. It is important to reflect on the available statistical evidence. From April 1999 to March 2004 2,497 ASBOs were applied for throughout England and Wales. Only 42 were refused by the courts giving a 98.3% success rate. It is clear that the lower burden of proof, the admission of hearsay evidence, the use of professional witnesses and easily convinced magistrates each contributed to this high success rate. The overall figure, however, was not evenly distributed over the five years. In the 12 months to March 2004 more ASBOs were issued than in the preceding four years taken together and there was a 60% drop in refusals. Those local authorities that use ASBOs most regularly proportionately had the lowest rate of refusals in the courts.

Throughout the five year period 74% of all ASBOs were issued against under 21s and of these 93% were to boys or young men. 49% of all ASBOs were issued against children aged 10 to 17. Between June 2000 and December 2002, the most recent figures available, of those young people prosecuted and found guilty of breaching their ASBO 50% were sentenced to a Young Offenders' Institution. The Home Office has not provided current information on breaches. Given the increase by a factor of five in the issuing of ASBOs between April 2003 and March 2004 it is fair to project the previous figures on breaches and custodial sentences by a similar factor. This would suggest 300 to 400 custodial sentences each year for breach. Put another way, these are children and young people who receive a custodial sentence having not been charged with a crime other than a breach of a civil injunction.

The Northern Ireland context

'ASBOs were introduced to meet a gap in dealing with persistent unruly behaviour, mainly by juveniles, and can be used against any person aged 10 or over.' (NIO 2004:4)

It is instructive that when the Northern Ireland Office (NIO) published its consultation document, Measures to Tackle Anti-social Behaviour in Northern Ireland, it misrepresented the initial focus of ASBOs, making it appear that they were directed primarily towards children. The brief and limited consultation was predicated on a previous consultation (NIO 2002) and strategy document (NIO 2003) each entitled Creating a Safer Northern Ireland Through Partnership. The consultation paper 'used recorded crime data, research findings on victimisation and the fear of crime, and consultation with key people working in community safety, to identify specific issues which needed to be addressed' (NIO 2002). From this, 'street violence, low level neighbourhood disorder and anti-social behaviour', emerged as significant and the resultant community safety strategy 'identified that the legislation in England and Wales on anti-social behaviour needed to be examined to see if it was appropriate for Northern Ireland' (NIO 2003). ASBOs were to be given particular consideration.

The 2004 consultation also included the proposed introduction of Anti-Social Behaviour Contracts (ABCs). Three specific measures were proposed. First, the development of Contracts as a non-statutory intervention, which might provide a sufficient warning to people considered to be involved in anti-social behaviour. For children it would involve parents or carers and could be used as a precursor to enforceable interventions. Second, the introduction of ASBOs as an option in cases where there already has been a conviction for a related criminal offence. Third, the use of ASBOs without any related criminal offence administered through a partnership between the police, district councils and the Northern Ireland Housing Executive.

Considerable controversy surrounded the consultation and the children's sector was united in its opposition to the introduction of ASBOs. The Northern Ireland Commissioner for Children and Young People (NICCY), with support from the leading children's NGOs challenged the proposed legislation on several grounds, not least the lack of consultation with children and young people. In rejecting the application the Judge concluded:

> *'... one wonders in practical and realistic terms what meaningful response could be obtained from children unless they were in a position to understand the legal and social issues to anti-social behaviour, the mechanisms for dealing with it. The shortcomings of existing criminal law and the effectiveness or otherwise of the English legislation and its suitability for transplant to the Northern Ireland context, and the interaction of Convention and international obligations [sic].'*

The Anti-Social Behaviour (Northern Ireland) Act was introduced on 25 August 2004. At no point was any reference made to the circumstances unique to Northern Ireland. The fact that anti-social behaviour, particularly that of children and young people, has been identified as an issue within communities was taken as sufficient justification to introduce legislation that is already controversial in terms of children's rights breaches in England and Wales. No serious consideration was given to the success of restorative justice and youth conferencing approaches in Northern Ireland and the potential disruption of those approaches through the introduction of a more directly punitive and criminal justice oriented mechanism. In its well argued submission to the Consultation an umbrella children's organisation observed that ASBOs have 'the potential to demonise and further exclude vulnerable children who already find themselves on the margins of society and the communities in which they live' (Include Youth 2004:5).

Further, and carrying potentially serious consequences, is the relationship of ASBOs to paramilitary punishments of children. For ASBOs and evictions have been introduced in circumstances where naming, shaming, beatings, shootings and exiling already exist regardless of their effectiveness. As a children's NGO focus group concluded: 'It's seen and represented as justice. It's concrete and immediate ... a quick fix. It doesn't work. It's brutal, inhuman and ineffective and doesn't challenge anti-social behaviour' (research focus group, Belfast, May 2004). Negotiations are already well developed within communities regarding paramilitary and vigilante interventions in the lives of children and young people. It is within this delicate climate, a process of real transition that anti-social behaviour legislation has been imposed. Additionally, as the Human Rights Commission (2004:8) noted: 'Information regarding the identity, residence and activities of those subject to an order [will] be in the public domain and could lead to the breach of a right to life were paramilitaries to act on that information'.

Within a month of their introduction the following unattributed poster appeared in East Belfast:

'DUE TO THE RECENT UPSURGE OF ANTI-SOCIAL BEHAVIOUR AND THE VERBAL AND MENTAL ABUSE ENDURED ON A DAILY BASIS BY THE ELDERLY PEOPLE IN THE SURROUNDING AREA YOU ARE FOREWARNED IF THIS DOES NOT STOP FORTHWITH IT WILL LEAVE US WITH NO ALTERNATIVE BUT TO DEAL WITH THE SITUATION AS WE DEEM NECESSARY NOTE: NO FURTHER WRITTEN OR VERBAL WARNING WILL BE GIVEN BE WARNED'

A research focus group (May 2004) concluded that 'Supporting ASBOs and supporting paramilitary beatings are derived in the same emotion: they're about revenge'.

The debate over the continuing conflict in Northern Ireland, particularly regarding the control of the streets and public space within communities returns the analysis to context. Hillyard et al (2003:29) make the important point regarding poverty:

> '... *the impact on the development and opportunities of these 150,000 children and young people [living in poverty] should not be underestimated. The wider consequences and costs for society as a whole must be a concern. These children and young people occupy ... "spaces of dispossession", growing up as excluded people in excluded families increasingly characterised by anti-social behaviour, insecurity and threat.*'

Children in Northern Ireland in conflict with the law cannot be viewed as simply manifesting anti-social behaviour in a form and content that is consistent with children in Liverpool, Glasgow, Birmingham, Dublin or Limerick. Their behaviours are rooted in the recent history of the conflict. The following comments, from community-based or children's sector NGO workers are typical:

> '*These are children of those whose childhood was dominated by the Troubles. We're talking about the experiences of children: house arrests, military presence, parents imprisoned, parents on the run, parents shot and killed. No allowances have been made in school. These experiences and their lasting effects aren't recognised.*
>
> *House-raids have lessened and the physical harm is over, to a point, but emotional harm is still there. Children and their parents are in dire need of medical support. The children are accused of misbehaving, of anti-social behaviour rather than their mental ill-health being recognised.*
>
> *Whether it's anti-social behaviour or suicidal tendencies, you cannot disconnect that from the anger of death in the communities. Shoot-to-kill, plastic bullets, collusion ... these are the experiences. Children often took over running of the home. The physical and psychological impact means these children have never been able to take their place in society. Transgenerational trauma affects every part of their lives: education, mental health, social participation. And in schools, in criminal justice agencies, trauma is not even part of the equation.*'

Without taking these dynamics into account and contextualising the perceived and experienced anti-social behaviour of children and young people in Northern Ireland's most economically marginalised communities, the authoritarianism of ASBOs as they have been administered in England and Wales has the potential to feed into that which already exists. It also has the potential to corrode the significant advances in alternatives to the 'criminal justice' option in undermining, both in philosophy and political direction, youth conferencing, parent support and restorative justice. They are incompatible with the draconian measures that constitute the armoury of the ever-expanding punishment industry.

The Gil-Robles Report

In June 2005 Alvaro Gil-Robles, European Human Rights Commissioner, reported on his visit to the United Kingdom 'on the effective respect of human rights in the country' (Gil-Robles 2005:4). Reflecting on the 'range of civil orders designed to combat low level crime and general nuisance' he focused on the ASBO which he identified as being 'particularly problematic' (ibid:34). He raised four principal concerns: '[t]he ease of obtaining such orders, the broad range of prohibited behaviour, the publicity surrounding their imposition and the serious consequences of breach ...'(ibid). While accepting the principle of civil orders, such as restraining orders, that 'protect an identifiable person or group ... from clearly specifiable behaviour on the part of another', 'the multiplication of civil orders in the United Kingdom ... are intended to protect not just specific individuals, but entire communities'. Their scope, in terms of the types of behaviour against which ASBOs are targeted, could be excessive and 'conditional on the subjective views of any collective'. Noting that the breach of an ASBO is a criminal offence with 'potentially serious consequences', he was concerned that 'the terms of orders' were defined in terms that 'invite[d] inevitable breach'. ASBOs were 'like personalised penal codes, where non-criminal behaviour becomes criminal for individuals who have incurred the wrath of the community'.

Gil-Robles was 'surprised by the enthusiasm' of the executive and legislature for 'this novel extension of civil orders'. He questioned 'the appropriateness of empowering local residents to take such matters into their own hands' particularly as this constituted 'the main selling point of ASBOs in the eyes of the executive' (ibid:35). He proposed that the main purpose of ASBOs was 'more to reassure the public that something is being done ... than the actual prevention of anti-social behaviour itself' (ibid). In this context the impression given was that the ASBO was 'touted as a miracle cure for urban nuisance'. This placed the police, local authorities and others 'under considerable pressure to apply for ASBOs' and magistrates similarly pressured 'to grant them'. 'The Commissioner 'hoped' for some respite from the 'burst of ASBO-mania with civil orders "limited to appropriate and serious cases".' This would be dependent on '[r]esponsible guidelines and realistic rhetoric'. Gil-Robles contested the expansion of ASBOs to include direct applications by individuals or groups and proposed 'responsible screening' of applications by a 'responsible authority' as a 'minimum guarantee against excessive use'.

Significantly he raised the issue of the appropriate standard of proof required for determining anti-social behaviour. While recognising the House of Lords judgment that the criminal standard of proof should apply, he noted that it accepted the admissibility of hearsay evidence because proceedings are civil. He found 'the combination of a criminal burden of proof with civil rules of evidence rather hard to square' and doubted that 'hearsay evidence and the testimony of police officers and professional witnesses' could 'be capable of proving the alleged behaviour beyond reasonable doubt' (ibid:36). If, as had been claimed, the rationale behind admitting hearsay evidence was to challenge witness intimidation the cases in question would constitute 'serious and actual harassment'. 'It is unfortunate', he continued, 'that ASBO proceedings are drawn up in such a way as to permit a range of behaviour that is merely disapproved of ... to be brought within their scope'. He concluded that Home Office Guidelines on targeted behaviour and evidence required 'unduly encourage the use of professional witnesses and hearsay evidence' while failing to 'emphasise the seriousness of the nuisance targeted'.

Gil-Robles, troubled that children between 10 and 14 could be considered 'criminally culpable' for their actions (ibid:33), was profoundly concerned that ASBOs brought children to the 'portal of the criminal justice system' (ibid:36). Reporting 'numerous complaints of excessive, victimising ASBOs' served on children, he proposed that such use was 'more likely to exacerbate anti-social behaviour and crime'. With a considerable number of children imprisoned for breaching orders and high reconviction rates for young offenders, he noted that the 'detention of juveniles for non-criminal behaviour' could 'lead to more serious offending on release' (ibid:37). The stigmatisation of children and their consequent, inevitable alienation ran the risk of further 'entrenching ... their errant behaviour'. He expressed surprise that widespread publicity of cases involving children was central to Home Office guidelines.

He concluded:

> *'It seems to me ... to be entirely disproportionate to aggressively inform members of the community who have no knowledge of the offending behaviour, and who are not affected by it, of the application of ASBOs ... they have no business and no need to*

know ... The aggressive publication of ASBOs, through, for instance the door step distribution of leaflets containing photos and addresses of children subject to ASBOs risks transforming the pesky into pariahs. The impact on the family as a whole must also be considered. Such indiscriminate naming and shaming would ... not only be counter-productive, but also a violation of Article 8 of the ECHR. Stricter guidelines and greater restraint would reduce the risk in practice and are urgently necessary.' (ibid:37)

While not calling for the abolition of ASBOs, Gil-Robles made five significant recommendations. These were: clear guidelines to delimit the behaviour targeted; no ASBOs to be issued on hearsay evidence alone; no expansion of recognised applicants for ASBOs to be made; no children under 16 to be imprisoned for breach of ASBOs; restrictions on excessive publicity and the prohibition of the reproduction and public dissemination of posters and photographs of children.

Concluding comment

This paper has argued that under the auspices of interagency co-operation and the promotion of 'collective responsibility', the veneer of risk, protection and prevention coats a deepening, almost evangelical, commitment to discipline, regulation and punishment. As the grip tightens on the behaviour of children and young people minimal attention has been paid to social, political and economic context. The reality is one in which authoritarian ideology has been mobilised locally and nationally to criminalise through the back door of civil injunctions. In-depth, case-based research already indicates that the problems faced by children and families are exacerbated by the stigma, rumour and reprisals fed by the very public process of naming and shaming.

ASBOs have been extended to the jurisdictions of Scotland and Northern Ireland and will be introduced in the Irish Republic. Despite a series of legal challenges, their continuing refinement and expansion of powers continues unabated. Yet they constitute serious breaches of the United Nations Convention on the Rights of the Child. In general these include: undermining of the 'best interests' principle, of the presumption of innocence, of 'due process', of the right to a fair trial and of access to legal representation. More specifically are breaches of Article 9 (separation from parents and the right to family life), of Article 13 (freedom of expression), of Article 15 (freedom of association) and of Article 16 (the protection of privacy).

Given the North of Ireland context and the risk of paramilitary beatings Article 6 (the right to life, survival and development) and Article 19 (protection from abuse and neglect) are, at best, compromised.

Further, it is evident that by imprisoning children for breaching ASBOs in England and Wales there is egregious breach of Article 40. In the context of Article 40, ASBOs do nothing to promote 'the child's sense of dignity and worth', have no consideration of age and limit the possibility of 'reintegration' into the community (Art 40.1). They conflate civil law and 'penal law' (Art 40.2a), compromise the presumption of innocence (Art 40.2bi), deny access to a 'fair hearing' (Art 40.biii), prevent cross examination of all witnesses whose evidence is before the court (Art 40.biv) and fail to respect privacy at all stages of the proceedings (Art 40.bvii). Imprisonment for breach of a civil order cannot be in keeping with the principle of depriving a child's liberty as a last resort. Nor does it deal with children 'in a manner appropriate to their well-being and proportionate both to their circumstances and the offence'. Finally, significant child protection issues are raised by publicly naming and shaming children as young as 10. Taken together, these breaches and circumstances amount to the most serious attack on children's rights since the UK Government ratified the Convention.

Acknowledgements

Many thanks to the participants in the Human Rights Commission seminar on antisocial behaviour in April 2004 and to those who attended sessions at other conferences, particularly the European Group for the Study of Deviance and Social Control at the University of Bristol in September 2004. I am deeply grateful for the critical comments of Deena Haydon and her participation in and co-authorship of earlier work. I am also grateful to those who participated in the research projects in North-West England and Northern Ireland.

The earlier sections of this paper are adaptations in part of a published article: 'Streets of Terror: Marginalisation, Criminalisation and Authoritarian Renewal' *Social Justice* vol.31, nos 1-2, 2004.

Phil Scraton is professor of criminology, Queens University, Belfast.

Footnotes

1 The UN Rules for the Protection of Juveniles deprived of their Liberty, 1990; the UN Standard Minimum Rules for the Administration of Juvenile Justice – the Beijing Rules, 1985; the UN Guidelines for the Prevention of Juvenile Delinquency – the Riyadh Guidelines, 1990; the UN Standard Minimum Rules for non-custodial measures –the Tokyo Rules, 1990.

2 These interviews were carried out within the Centre for Studies in Crime and Social Justice, Edge Hill University College. With thanks to Donna Lawrenson and Julie Read.

References

Allen R 1999 'Is What Works What Counts? The Role of Evidence-based Crime Reduction in Policy and Practice' Safer Society vol 2

Ashworth A, Gardner J, Morgan R, Smith A T H, von Hirsch A and Wasik M 1998 'Neighbouring on the oppressive: the Government's 'Antisocial behaviour order' Criminal Justice 16, 7-14

Audit Commission 1996 Misspent Youth: Young People and Crime London, Audit Commission

Blair T 2000 'My vision for Britain' Observer 10 November

Freeman M 2000 'The Future of Children's Rights' Children and Society vol 14 (3), pp277-293

Gardner J, von Hirsch A, Smith A T H, Morgan R, Ashworth A and Wasik M 'Clause 1 – The Hybrid Law from Hell' Criminal Justice Matters, 31

Garland D 1996 'The limits of the sovereign state' British Journal of Criminology vol 36, no 4, 445-471

Gil-Robles A 2005 Report by Mr Alvaro Gil-Robles, Commissioner for Human Rights, on his Visit to the United Kingdom, 4th-12th November 2004 Strasbourg, Office of the Commissioner for Human Rights

Goldson B 1997 'Children in Trouble: State Responses to Juvenile Crime' in P Scraton (ed) 'Childhood' in 'Crisis'? London, UCL Press 124-145

Goldson B 2000 'Wither Diversion? Interventionism and the New Youth Justice' in B. Goldson (ed) The New Youth Justice Dorset, Russell House

Gould P 1998 The Unfinished Revolution: How the Modernizers Saved the Labour Party London, Little Brown

Haydon D and Scraton P 2000 '"Condemn a Little More, Understand a little less": The political context and rights implications of the domestic and European rulings in the Venables-Thompson case' Journal of Law and Society vol 27, no 3, 416-448

Hester R 2000 'Community Safety and the new youth justice' in B Goldson (ed) The New Youth Justice Lyme Regis, Russell House

Hillyard P, Kelly G, McLaughlin E, Patsios D, and Tomlinson M 2003 Bare Necessities: poverty and social exclusion in Northern Ireland – key findings Belfast, Democratic Dialogue 16

Home Office 1998 Crime and Disorder Act 1998: Introductory Guide London, Home Office Communication Directorate

Human Rights Commission 2004 'Measures to Tackle Anti- Social Behaviour in Northern Ireland': The Response of the Northern Ireland Human Rights Commission Belfast, NIHRC

Include Youth 2004 Response to Measures to Tackle Anti- Social Behaviour in Northern Ireland Consultation Document Belfast, Include Youth

Johnston G and Bottomley A K 1998 'Introduction: Labour's Crime Policy in Context' Policy Studies vol 19, no 3/4

Lawrenson D 2002 'The Crime and disorder Act 1998: Young People and their Parents'/ Carers' Experiences of the Law' Unpublished Dissertation Centre for Studies in Crime and Social Justice, Edge Hill

Liverpool ASBU 2002 Liverpool Anti-Social Behaviour Unit: Draft Strategy Liverpool, ASBU March

Local Government Information Unit 1997 Community Safety: Consultation in Advance of the Crime and Disorder Bill London, Home Office

Muncie J 1999 'Institutionalized intolerance: youth justice and the 1998 Crime and Disorder Act' Critical Social Policy vol 19, no 2, 147-175

NIO 2002 'Creating a Safer Northern Ireland Through Partnership': A Consultative Paper Belfast, Community Safety Unit NIO, April

NIO 2003 'Creating a Safer Northern Ireland Through Partnership': A Strategy Document Belfast, Community Safety Unit, NIO, March

NIO 2004 Measures to Tackle Anti-Social Behaviour in Northern Ireland: A Consultation Document Belfast, Criminal Justice Policy Branch NIO

Pitts J 2001 The New Politics of Youth Crime: Discipline or Solidarity? Basingstoke, Palgrave

Scraton P 1997 'Whose 'Childhood'? What 'Crisis'?' in P Scraton (ed) 'Childhood' in 'Crisis'? London, UCL Press

Scraton P 2002a 'The Demonisation, Exclusion and Regulation of Children: From Moral Panic to Moral Renewal' in A. Boran (ed) Crime: fear or fascination? Chester, Chester Academic Press, 9-39

Scraton P 2002b 'The Politics of Morality' in P Scraton (ed) Beyond September 11: An Anthology of Dissent London, Pluto Press, 40-46

Scraton P 2004 'Streets of Terror: Marginalisation, Criminalisation and Moral Renewal' Social Justice vol.31, nos 1-2. pp130-158

UK Government 1999 Convention on the Rights of the Child: Second Report to the UN Committee on the Rights of the Child London, Department of Health

YJB/CYPU 2002 Establishing Youth Inclusion and Support Panels (YISPS): Draft Guidance Note for Children's Fund Partnerships and Youth Offending Teams London, Youth Justice Board

14

The state of ASBO Britain – the rise of intolerance

Max Rowlands

Anti-Social Behaviour Orders (ASBOs) have become the cornerstone of New Labour's campaign to restore a culture of 'respect' to British society. Introduced seven years ago, but little used before the last four, they have become increasingly popular among both the agencies in charge of their application and the general public (a June 2005 MORI poll showed that 82% of people support their use[1]). And, yet while every set of government statistics reports a proportional rise in the number being issued, and anecdotal evidence in the press indicates a steady growth of behaviour deemed incorporable under the antisocial 'umbrella', there has been very little public debate regarding their appropriateness and effectiveness.

The reality is that ASBOs are being used far beyond their initial remit of dealing with vandals and nuisance neighbours. Behaviour that is overtly non-criminal is being criminalised and society's vulnerable groups are being targeted. Increasingly it is behaviour that is different rather than 'antisocial' that is being penalised. The form such punishment takes is perhaps of even greater concern because ASBOs effectively bypass criminal law and operate within their own shadow legal system. In effect, we no longer need to break the law to go to jail. In this sense they typify a growing abandonment of the rule of law that writers such as Magnus Hörnqvist have warned against[2]. They reflect a blurring of the distinction between crime and nuisance behaviour that has resulted in greater significance being placed in how objectionable behaviour is, rather than how lawful. It is on this basis that the previously tolerable behaviour of minority groups, such as beggars, the homeless and travellers, is being targeted.

What are ASBOs?

ASBOs were introduced under the Crime and Disorder Act (1998) and have since been significantly amended by the Police Reform Act (2002) and the Anti-Social Behaviour Act (2003). Orders can ban any individual over ten years of age both from carrying out specific acts and from entering certain geographical areas for a minimum period of two years. They can be applied for by police forces (including the British Transport Police), local authorities, housing action trusts and registered social landlords to a magistrates' court or county court. The decision whether or not to make the order is made at a full court hearing but, because ASBOs are intended as a 'quick-fire' solution to immediate problems within a community, an interim order can be made ahead of it. A typical order contains multiple restrictions to an individual's movement and actions along with the general stipulation that they must not cause 'alarm or distress' to others. In some cases a curfew is also imposed. The scope and jurisdiction of each order can vary dramatically. In some an individual will be banned from carrying out a specific act throughout the whole of England and Wales, in others the restriction is limited to within the local authority's boundaries. There is similar variation in geographical restrictions, with bans ranging from streets to cities to counties. There are multiple cases of individuals being banned from their own home[3]. In short, the applying body can concoct virtually any set of restrictions it deems fit.

ASBOs can also be made on conviction in criminal proceedings where the defendant is made subject to an order in addition to their sentence. There is no formal application process for this, so usually the Crown Prosecution Service asks the court to impose the order. Although coming into effect on the day it is made, it is possible for the court to suspend its prohibitions until the offender is released from custody. Orders on conviction, despite often being somewhat erroneously referred to as 'criminal ASBOs' or 'CRASBOs', are, along with all forms of ASBOs, civil orders. This means that in their application process hearsay evidence is admissible in court and there is no jury. This, together with the government's loose definition of 'anti-social behaviour' as that 'which causes or is likely to cause harassment, alarm or distress', has facilitated an extraordinarily high success rate in the application process. For the 2,455 orders issued by the end of March 2004, only 42 requests were turned down by the courts[4]. This is a disturbing statistic when you consider both that breaching an ASBO is a criminal offence, punishable by up to five years in prison for adults and a two-year detention and training order for children, and that their use continues to rise rapidly. Nearly 20 per cent of the 3,826 orders issued between April 1999 and September 2004 were made between July and September 2004[5]. The most recent Home Office statistics illustrate a similar quarterly rise with the total number at 4,649 by December 2004[6]. 42 percent of

145

those given ASBOs will breach their order, of which just over half will then receive custodial sentences[7].

In terms of distribution ASBOs are a geographical lottery. Manchester has issued five times more orders than Liverpool (where fear of anti-social behaviour is lower and has fallen faster than in its neighbouring city), while the borough of Camden is responsible for around a third of the whole of London's[8]. Increasingly the qualification for whether your behaviour merits an order depends on the enthusiasm for them of your local council. This worsens the potential for manipulation already inherent in the admissibility of hearsay evidence. A woman in Wales was cleared of seven charges of breaching her order, all of which were made by her neighbours. Another in Dagenham claimed that her ASBO was based on the lies of a malicious neighbour with whom she had been involved in a long running dispute: 'The only reason I was in court rather than her was because she got to the police first'.

The potential for abuse is just as strong once an order has been made because the police are dependent on the cooperation of local communities for their effective enforcement. In Peterborough, the city council even offered people CCTV cameras and dictaphones to gather evidence against their neighbours. ASBO recipients are also frequently 'named and shamed' with their name, photograph and the terms of their order distributed in leaflets, published in the local press and posted on the internet. A June 2005 report by the Council of Europe's human rights commissioner, Alvaro Gil-Robles, believed this practice to be a breach of human rights[9]. Whole families become stigmatised and at risk of vigilante attacks. For example, in Chester up to 30 youths vandalised the house a 49-year-old ASBO holder shares with his brother and mother.

Britain appears to be in the grip of 'Asbomania' (to use Gil-Robles' term). Certainly the absorption of orders into mainstream culture is increasingly evident. In June 2005 the word 'Asbo' was both added to the Collins English Dictionary, and recognised as a pet dog name. More importantly it has become the knee-jerk reaction for anyone in dispute over another's supposedly unreasonable behaviour. A Halifax Pet Insurance survey found that four out five people wanted ASBOs to be given to the owners of illmannered pets. In Harlow, residents angry at the state of their area's recycling bins have tried to serve their council an order. It is on this growing wave of intolerance that Bluewater shopping centre's ban on hooded tops was widely welcomed. Orders have served to alter perceptions of what behaviour is tolerable and become a blanket solution for any social dispute.

And yet despite these dangers, the government seems intent on making it even easier to serve them. The Home Office strategic plan 'Confident Communities in a Secure Britain', published in July 2004, both sped up the application process and made it easier for the media to report ASBO recipients. In July 2005, changes to the application process, originally outlined by Lord Chancellor Lord Falconer in October 2004, came into force under section 143 of the Serious Organised Crime and Police Act (2005). Witnesses are now able to give evidence from behind screens and by video link and use intermediaries when communicating with the police. These practices, although not new, have previously been confined to use in criminal proceedings. Legal distinctions between the two are being eroded.

The use of ASBOs

Writing in *Race & Class*, Magnus Hörnqvist argues that the rule of law has been weakened through the blurring of lines between criminal acts and minor public order offences. Further, what constitutes crime is being redefined. He highlights the 'European Council decision setting up a European crime prevention network' in which crime is said to include 'anti-social conduct which, without necessarily being a criminal offence, can by its cumulative effect generate a climate of tension and insecurity'[10]. Under this fudging, Hörnqvist argues, crime is no longer synonymous with penal law breaches. It is now security, rather than the law, that dictates the use of force in society. The 'undesirable behaviours' that governments are increasingly intervening against have been defined not through their accordance with the law but the perception of what generates (feelings of) insecurity. The effect of this is that:

> *'At the most fundamental level, the focus is shifted to what a person might do instead of what a person has done. The central question to be asked in the context of a possible intervention is not "has this individual committed a crime?" but, rather, "does this person constitute a risk?"' (pp.37)*

ASBOs can best be understood as part of a movement away from the rule of law, democratic standards and the fundamental notion that we will not be punished if we abide by our society's penal code. Under its simplistic mandate virtually any behaviour can now become criminal if someone can convince a court that it has caused them either to be alarmed or distressed. The effect of this is that we now have in place a shadow legal system that is criminalising more behaviour by the day. Being sarcastic, using the word 'Taliban', feeding birds in your garden – all of these actions, outlawed by ASBOs in three separate cases, are now capable of incurring prison terms for their holders. But while these extreme examples achieve notoriety and grab the headlines of the national press, it is the quieter, more underhand targeting of society's vulnerable minority groups that is of greatest concern.

Home Office guidelines for the Crime and Disorder Act stated that ASBOs would be issued to children only in 'exceptional circumstances', but in practice just over half of all orders made between June 2000 and March 2004 have been[11]. Individuals as young as ten are criminalised for their anti-social behaviour, examples of which include playing football in the street, riding a bike, wearing a hood and using the word 'grass'. 'Naming and shaming' is also particularly damaging in these cases; a stigma, at such an early age, that will not easily wear off. The children's charity, Barnardo's, says 'all experience suggests that children who gain status from poor behaviour are much more likely to continue with the behaviour if they are publicly labelled'[12]. In July 2005, Section 141 of the Serious Organised Crime and Police Act came into force and continued this trend by removing a child's right to automatic anonymity when they appear in a youth court charged with a breach of their ASBO. Further, these methods of publicising cases clearly contravene Article 40 of the United Nations Convention on the Rights of the Child which provides a guarantee for each 'to have his or her privacy fully respected.'

And for those children whose behaviour really does call for state intervention ASBOs are proving to be an ineffective remedy. There are frequent media reports of orders being treated as little more than a 'badge of honour'. In one instance a boy in a local authority secure unit proudly pasted local media coverage of his order on the walls of his room. Such cases totally undermine the ASBO's intended role as a deterrent. Indeed, with 42% of all orders being breached in 2004, this led to nearly 50 children being admitted to custody every month[13].

There is also significant potential for victimisation as highlighted by information given to Statewatch detailing three cases in Wales. The families of one 15 and two 16-year-old boys all alleged that the police have been circulating photos of their sons and asking local residents if they have caused disturbances or been guilty of anti-social acts. All feel that their children are being unfairly targeted by a police force intent on making examples. The implications of this kind of harassment, in conjunction with the fact that, to date, 98.3% of ASBO applications have been successful, are highly disturbing. One can only speculate as to how many orders have been made under similar circumstances (to both adults and children), but the potential for manipulation and the settling of vendettas is clearly evident.

Equally alarming is an August 2005 report by the British Institute for Brain Injured Children which details more than 15 cases where children with Asperger's, Tourette's Syndrome and Attention Deficit Hyperactivity Disorder have been given ASBOs. They warn that there are numerous similar cases. Many of these children cannot properly understand the orders they have been given and yet face custody if they persist in non-criminal behaviour such as staring over a neighbour's fence and bouncing on a trampoline. Incredibly a child with Tourette's syndrome (a neurological disorder that can cause the involuntary use of obscene words) has been banned from swearing in public. Adults with mental health problems have been similarly targeted. In February 2005, a well-publicised order was made against a 23-year-old woman who had attempted to commit suicide on four occasions. She was banned from any river, watercourse or canal in England and Wales, and from loitering on bridges or going onto railway tracks. The behaviour of those with personality disorders has also often been met with an ASBO. This use of orders has received universal condemnation from organisations working in the field of mental health. Richard Brook, chief executive of Mind, said, 'It is completely inappropriate for those experiencing mental distress to potentially be criminalised rather than receiving the support they so desperately need'[14].

The scope of ASBOs has also extended to combat a wide range of public order offences. Many prostitutes, beggars, homeless people and those with drug and alcohol addiction problems have found themselves barred from the areas they frequent. In August 2005 a homeless man was jailed for three weeks for sitting at the bottom of a fire escape behind a derelict building. In March 2005, a drug addict, who turned to begging to fund his habit, was jailed for three months under the terms of his order for 'courteously' asking a motorcyclist for money. A homeless man in Birmingham, forbidden from begging, breached his order and was jailed for two years. Having served eight months he was released but soon breached the order again and was this time jailed for three years – a total of five years custody for a non-criminal offence. Early in 2005, a Manchester prostitute was given an order prohibiting her from carrying condoms in the same area that her drug clinic was based (which provided them to her as part of its harm-reduction strategy). She breached the order and was put on probation[15]. Many others prostitutes have been jailed despite loitering and solicitation being non-imprisonable for over ten years.

These examples represent just the tip of an iceberg and have led to increasing criticism from charities working in relevant fields. The housing charity Shelter has expressed concern that being given an ASBO can lead to eviction and exclusion from housing, whether it is breached or not, because it may violate a tenancy agreement. Further, the social stigma attached to an order may lead a landlord to decide that they are undesirable tenants and evict them. The homeless charity Crisis fears that 'ASBOs will create even more obstacles to people obtaining the services they desperately need'[16]. And the manager of Trust, a community project supporting sex workers in south London, warned that they do nothing to improve the housing and drug problems that invariably force women into prostitution. Instead orders serve to make life more dangerous by forcing many to take greater risks so as to avoid the attention of local authorities[17].

Typical of ASBOs, this targeting of the symptom and not the cause does nothing to help people who live in poverty and are driven to their anti-social behaviour through desperation. Those who have no choice but to beg or solicit themselves must choose between relocating to an area outside the order's jurisdiction or risk incarceration should they be caught breaching it. Historically these social problems have occupied a grey area in criminal law, but in the parallel legal system created by ASBOs, the government can evade the difficulty of legally defining these sensitive issues. Instead, local authorities now have the opportunity to displace their undesirable elements to their neighbours. Travellers seem to have recently joined this list after an order made in August 2005 established a five mile exclusion zone which a family of travellers could not inhabit, thus setting a precedent for their use in this field.

The government has also tried to categorise the act of political protest as anti-social. In May 2005 the police and Ministry of Defence were unsuccessful in acquiring an ASBO against a 63- year-old peace campaigner protesting outside a US listening base at Menworth Hill, though this may, in part, be because the case received a great deal of publicity. This prompted a member of the House of Lords to ask whether Parliament could ever have envisaged that ASBOs would 'be used by government agencies who find a particular protest annoying or embarrassing'[18]. In February 2005, a council tenant who put antiwar leaflets through 50 of his neighbours' letterboxes was threatened with eviction and given an 'anti-social behaviour interview' which he was told could lead to an ASBO. And in August 2004 two protesters and a baby were prevented from holding a banner and handing out leaflets outside Reed Exhibitions, the organiser of DSEi (Defence Systems and Equipment International), the world's largest arms fair. Police applied for a temporary ASBO to order their dispersal. Animal rights activists have also been targeted with a seemingly high percentage of successful applications made against them.

Other areas of the law designed to combat anti-social behaviour have also been inappropriately used in this field. In June 2004, when nine Palestine solidarity campaigners staged a peaceful protest outside Caterpillar's Solihull offices against the company's continued sale of bulldozers to the Israeli military they were told by police that they were believed to be acting in an anti-social manner and as such must provide them with their names and addresses. When asked for the legal basis of this assertion the police were unable to provide them with the correct Act, let alone its appropriate section (it is Section 50 of the Police Reform Act). The protestors refused to comply and were subsequently arrested (although Section 50 carries no specific power of arrest). When their case came to trial in early 2005 the charges were dropped. A number of the activists are now suing the police for illegal arrest, unlawful detention and malicious prosecution. In September 2005, anti-DSEi protestors shifted the focus of their attention up a level from the previous year and campaigned outside the offices of Reed Elsevier, the parent company of Reed Exhibitions. Whilst handing out leaflets to passers by, people were (incorrectly) told by police officers that the Anti Social Behaviour Act required them to provide their names and addresses. And under the Serious Organised Crime and Police Act, from 1 July 2005, all protestors must obtain police permission before staging a demonstration in the half-mile area around Westminster.

The legal context: a shadow system?
Orders made on conviction provide a clear example of how ASBOs have intruded on traditional areas of criminal law. The ASBO was intended as a preventative measure that would steer people away from damaging behaviour likely to lead to criminal charges, but orders on conviction (which make up 41% of all orders) represent no

more than a double punishment[19]. The implicit assumption behind them is that the individual is likely to re-offend upon release, a standpoint that totally undermines the idea of prison as a rehabilitative institution. Serious questions should be asked of the message recriminalising people, as soon as they have served their punishment, sends both to prospective employers and the individuals themselves about their prospects of reintegrating into society.

There are also many examples of ASBOs being used directly in place of the law. Because they are so easy to obtain and any behaviour can be outlawed, local authorities have increasingly used them to prohibit low-level offences that are already covered under the criminal law. The most extreme example of this practice is the case of a man in Birmingham who was banned from committing any crime in his borough. This extraordinary stipulation meant that, in theory, he could be imprisoned up to a maximum of five years for any minor criminal offence. The homeless man jailed for sitting on a fire escape had similar clauses in his order, one of which forbade him from shoplifting in West Yorkshire. When his probation officer phoned the government's anti-social behaviour unit to enquire as to the need for this restriction he was told that it was because the courts did not take shoplifting seriously. This he claimed to be a surprise given that he regularly deals with shoplifters sent to prison. He also noted that when issuing the order the court 'had gone down his extensive list of previous convictions and made everything he had ever been convicted of the subject of an ASBO. The fact that he had already been punished for these acts, often by long terms of imprisonment, was neither here nor there'[20].

Their reasons for doing this are twofold. Firstly, it is easier to secure convictions through an ASBO. Secondly, it means that any criminal offence is punishable by up to five years in prison. Clearly it should not be for council employees, civil servants or indeed the courts to decide that the criminal justice system is not up to its task. Accordingly two recent judgments found against this practice. In July 2005, a man who breached his order banning him from (the already criminal offence of) driving whilst disqualified had his sentence reduced from a year to the six-month maximum penalty the law allows. In doing so the judge ruled it 'wrong in principle' for ASBOs to be used simply for the purpose of increasing sentences[21]. In June 2005, an order that included a clause banning a child from committing any criminal offence in England or Wales was deemed plainly too wide and not 'necessary'[22].

Whether these cases will set a precedent and reduce the encroachment of ASBOs is uncertain, but the functions of 'traditional law' are undoubtedly under attack. 'Rough' or 'summary' justice, as Tony Blair refers to it, is spearheaded by the use of fixed penalty notices with which police officers, community support officers and accredited persons (which can include private security guards) can issue instant on-the-spot fines. According to Blair they are necessary because Britain's criminal justice system is 'too complicated, too laborious' and unable to 'get the job done'[23]. To this end, in an extraordinary statement in September 2005, he revealed that: 'Whatever powers the police need to crack down on this [anti-social behaviour], I will give them'[24].

Given this increasing subversion of due process, it is highly disturbing that those in charge of drafting and enforcing ASBOs do not fully understand their legal implications. In November 2004 a mother and her five children were evicted from their home after two of her sons breached their orders. Her local council, having initially refused to re-house them on the basis that they had made themselves 'intentionally homeless', was later forced to put them up in a hotel at a cost of over £8,000 when a county court judge ruled in her favour. Poor drafting is also evident both in the ASBO application process and in its official form. Solicitor Matt Foot, representing a beggar whom Camden council were attempting to ban from three London boroughs, described the evidence offered against him as 'fourth-hand hearsay'[25]. Unsurprisingly the aforementioned homeless man, jailed for sitting on a fire escape and recriminalised for every previous transgression, had no better luck with the drafting of his order of which some parts were unintelligible and others illegible in the form of hand-written unnumbered pasted in clauses. Other drafting errors have achieved comic status and include a man forbidden from not being drunk and an unborn baby threatened with an order. But of greatest concern is whether council employees have sufficient training and understanding of how ASBOs work. In March 2005 a four-year-old boy threw a toy at a council worker's car as she visited his family. His mother says that two days later the official returned and announced she wanted to give the child an ASBO.

Conclusion

Few would deny that a number of ASBO cases have warranted state intervention. The problem with using ASBOs here is that they don't work. Every set of government statistics has shown a progressive increase in the percentage being breached. With almost half currently not adhered to they hardly inspire confidence in their capacity to protect us. At the same time there is no direct statistical evidence to indicate a rise in 'anti-social behaviour' and the ever-increasing number of orders it has supposedly necessitated. What we do know is that while crime fell by 39% between 1995 and 2004 (the longest sustained drop since 1898)[26], over the same period of time the prison population rose by 25,000 people[27]. On 7 October 2005 it stood at 77,373, a gain of 3,270 inmates since the start of the year; an even steeper rise. In June 2005, the Howard League for Penal Reform warned that at the current rate we will require a new institution the size of Brixton prison every month just to maintain current levels of overcrowding[28].

Thus, in their intended role as a preventative measure that would reduce the necessity of incarceration, ASBOs have comprehensively failed. Again it is worth emphasising that around 50 children are jailed every month. The annual cost of incarcerating each child is £70,000. A case in Manchester appealed both at the High Court and the Court of Appeal eventually cost the council £187,700, while Metropolitan Police estimates cases costing as much as £100,000 should they be breached. Surely these vast sums of money could be better spent attempting to address the root causes of 'anti-social behaviour', such as by improving a local community's resources. In Wythenshawe, Manchester, there are two youth clubs for 8,000 young people.

Yet ASBOs remain popular and accordingly the extent to which they have pervaded British culture is of worry to civil libertarians. Previously the appropriate response to sensitive issues such as begging, homelessness, prostitution, travellers and youth crime was the subject of debate. There was recognition that these were social problems largely created by desperation and poverty, not criminal activity. The wholly inappropriate 'one size fits all' ASBO has removed this distinction. Now anything or anyone that causes others to be alarmed or distressed is targeted; whether the offending behaviour is criminal is irrelevant. And at every opportunity the government stokes the fire, telling us that we have more reason to feel alarmed and distressed than ever before; that children are out of control, 'lager louts' dominate town centres each weekend and our society is overrun by a 'culture of disrespect'.

Max Rowlands

But ASBOs do not level down people's fear of 'anti-social behaviour'; they exacerbate it. The more ASBOs are issued, the more the supposedly imminent threat 'anti-social behaviour' poses is in the news and the more obsessed with it people become. To this extent ASBOs are a self-fulfilling prophecy. Manchester has managed to issue significantly more orders than its neighbouring cities yet retain a population with a greater fear of anti-social behaviour. And as a result Britain, historically a country with pretensions towards the toleration of social and cultural differences, is becoming increasingly puritanical. ASBOs have given us new definitions of what is criminal, and stringent new guidelines of what is acceptable behaviour for a social being. In doing so they have also provided an outlet for intolerance. The toleration of others, within reason, has always been a part of social life. The consequence of ASBOs, intentional or not, has been to redefine the boundaries of what is deemed to be reasonable.

Max Rowlands is a volunteer researcher with Statewatch.

Foototes

1 MORI Social Research Institute survey, June 2005: http://www.mori.com/polls/2005/asbo.shtml
2 Magnus Hörnqvist, 'The birth of public order policy' in *Race & Class*, Volume 46 No.1, July-September 2004.
3 Details of all cases mentioned in this article can be found on Statewatch's ASBOwatch website: http://www.statewatch.org/asbo/ASBOwatch.html
4 Home Office statistics
5 Hazel Blears written ministerial statements, 1.03.05 http://www.theyworkforyou.com/wms/?id=2005-03-01.80WS.3
6 Home Office statistics: http://www.crimereduction.gov.uk/asbos2.htm
7 Charles Clarke, 'Yobs will face the consequences of their actions'. Home Office press release, 01.03.05: http://www.devon-cornwall.police.uk/v3/news/latest/pressrelease.cfm?id=92
8 Home Office statistics – op. cit. [6]
9 Alvaro Gil-Robles, 'Report by Mr Alvaro Gil-Robles, Commissioner for Human Rights, on his visit to the United Kingdom 4-12th November 2004', 08.06.05: http://www.statewatch.org/news/2005/jun/coe-ukreport. pdf
10 Council of the European Union, 'Council decision setting up a European crime prevention network' (26 April 2001, 7794/01)
11 Home Office statistics. See also: Independent 20.06.05 http://www.socialist–teacher.org/news.asp?d=y&id=552
12 Press release, 'Children and anti-social behaviour'. 18.02.05
13 Youth Justice Board statistics: http://www.youth-justice-board.gov.uk/

14 Richard Brook quoted in John Pring, 'Time for Last Orders' in *Disability Now*: http://www.disabilitynow.org.uk/people/opinion/newsfoc_jul2005.htm

15 'Anti Social Behaviour Orders: analysis of the first six years', NAPO (The trade union and professional association for family court and probation staff) briefing for the launch of Asbo Concern:
http://www.napo.org.uk/napolog2/archives/ASBOs%20analysis%20-%20briefing%20for%20luanch%20of%20ASBO%20Concern%207%20April.pdf

16 Crisis press office quote

17 Laura Smith, 'Asbos "are bringing back jail for prostitutes"', *Guardian*, 25.05.05: http://www.guardian.co.uk/uk_news/story/0,,1491329,00.html

18 Question asked by Baroness Miller of Chilthorne Domer, Lords Hansard text, 23.05.05: http://www.parliament.the-stationery-office.co.uk/pa/ld199900/ldhansrd/pdvn/lds05/text/50523-01.htm

19 Home Office statistics – op. cit. [7]

20 John Bell, 'Rough justice', *Guardian*, 10.08.05:
http://politics.guardian.co.uk/homeaffairs/story/0%2C11026%2C1545737%2C00.html.

21 BBC News Online, 'Court criticises driver's Asbo', 26.07.05: http://news.bbc.co.uk/2/hi/uk_news/england/west_midlands/4719315.stm

22 (W v Director of Public Prosecutions [2005] EWHC 1333 (Admin) Legal Action August 2005 pp19, *Times* 20.06.05

23 10 Downing Street press conference, 11.10.05. See also: *The Times* 12.10.05: http://www.timesonline.co.uk/article/0,,17129-1821908,00.html

24 Tony Blair, Labour conference speech, 29.09.05.

25 Matt Foot quoted in Andrew Gilligan, 'How the mania for Asbos is turning children into victims', *Evening Standard*, 15.08.05. Matt Foot is the national co-ordinator of Asbo Concern, a group campaigning for a full public government review of ASBOs.

26 Home Office Statistical Bulletin, 'Crime in England and Wales 2003/2004', July 2004: http://www.homeoffice.gov.uk/rds/pdfs04/hosb1004.pdf

27 Prison Reform Trust press release, 'England and Wales – Western Europe's Jail Capital', 2.02.04

28 The Howard League for Penal Reform press statement, 28.06.05: http://www.howardleague.org/press/2005/280605.pdf

15

Bulgaria –
the Microsoft contract

Gergana Jouleva & Alexander Kashumov

No, there is no mistake in the title. It came as a logical question after reading Decision No 6930 of the Five-member Panel of the Supreme Administrative Court (SAC) of Bulgaria as of 15 July 2005. The Decision was delivered on the case of Access to Information Programme (AIP) and two MPs versus the refusal of the Minister of State Administration to disclose the Bulgarian government contract with 'Microsoft' Corporation.

In 2002 the Minister purchased from the company about 30,000 software licenses for the Bulgarian public administration and paid 13,650 million dollars for them. He did not follow the public procurement procedure and *did not* present the contract to Parliament. Two MPs and AIP filed a request to the Minister and received a late response that the contract would be withheld in view of the lack of Microsoft Corporation consent.

In the first instance the court found the denial unlawful but after the Minister appealed the five-member panel of the Court declared the initial complaint inadmissible and dropped the proceedings. The Court's decision is final and cannot be appealed.

According to the Court judgment the law provides an opportunity to the responding authority to prolong the 14-days period for response up to 14 more days when a third party is concerned. In this case Microsoft Corporation interests were concerned. The complainants were obliged to know, even if not informed, that a third party would be asked for consent. The Court found that the complainants were challenged prematurely and were granted refusal[1] instead of waiting for a response within the prolonged time period. Consequently their complaint was declared inadmissible.

The case is similar to other access-to-information cases also involving state contracting for the customs reforms and highways concession. The common characteristics of all these requests-for-access-to-state-contracts cases are: large amounts of money paid, avoiding public procurement, invoking access to information exemptions to withhold information.

Besides the formalities, the Court decision states that the tax-payers have no right to see contracts between the state and private companies, even if the payments are from the state budget.

The Court decision is astounding in several ways. It makes the optimists who believe in the consistency of such decisions on access to information look like foolish and enthusiastic activists.

First, it came out that someone requesting access to documents has the duty to foresee, without any notice, any minister's intent to require the consent of a third party (in cases of public procurement this is usually the contractor) before disclosing the contract between the company and the state.

The question is then, what if a requester is confident that the contracts of the state with any company – aided by taxes – would be public under the law? These are, presumably, the practices in democratic countries especially with regard to contracts paid from the state budget. How could one predict whether a minister holds a different opinion and chooses to take his decision dependent on third party consent? These different views on the matter were the reason to refer the case to the Court, weren't they?

Second, the judges obviously believe that the Minister of State Administration did not deny information. He only gave it a bit later, because he was busy asking for the third party consent. In that case, the judges believed that the requesters would have been inexcusably impudent to appeal to the granted refusal of the minister instead of waiting for the written response. The latter was received late in the afternoon of the 28th day of the request submission (the last day for a possible appeal). This response in fact came after the complaint was sent to the Court. Its content was a short summary of the contract.

The question is now, what happens if the requesters did not want to miss the deadline for the submission of a complaint against the refusal? Why do the legally stipulated timeframes exist if not to enable the requester to know when to expect a response and when he has the right to appeal a refusal?

Third, the starting point of the Court judgment is a long observation of the question whether the Minister of State Administration was a body obliged by (covered by) the Access to Public Information Act (APIA) as it could be disputable. At least the finding was that the Minister was obliged. On the other hand, it was indisputable, to the court, that in this particular case, the information was about the activities of a private company, which was not obliged to provide access to public information since it was not financed through the state budget. Indeed, we would agree that it is indisputable firstly, that Microsoft Corporation is a private business company and, secondly, that this company is not financed by the state budget. It is unclear though, why this speculation was necessary when the requesters requested the information from the minister, not from the company, and the subject of the case was precisely the contract with the state.

When the court proceedings started there was a hope that it was indisputable that the Minister of State Administration was an obliged body under the law. It was indisputable that the Minister of State Administration was the institution responsible to society for the implementation of the Access to Public Information Act. These indisputable facts are even written down in the law.[2]

On the other hand, it was very much disputable that the public and the MPs have no right to see a contract between the state administration and private company, moreover one that had been paid by citizens' taxes.

Several issues are important here. If a public authority pays a private company, then we are usually talking about public procurement. If the tender procedure is avoided, a special public interest should stay behind the exception – national security or public order. When we are talking about private interest or a commercial interest, then again we are limiting all discussion to the scope of that interest. In democratic countries, the two interests are balanced against each other and if the public interest of disclosure overrides, the information should be released. In those countries it is apparent and indisputable that the decision should be in favour of the public interest, not of a private one. This applies especially, when the tender procedure has been avoided.

Someone may say, 'I beg your pardon, but Microsoft is the best company,' why do we need to follow the formalities, which would only make the process more expensive?

Maybe that is the reason why society needs to know – to shape their own opinion on the high quality of services Microsoft Corporation provides to the Bulgarian administration represented by the Minister of State Administration. Why is the best quality so jealously kept out of public eyes?

The case is over now. The Court delivered its decision. The second instance ruled in contradiction to its positive case-law on the Access to

Public Information Act that the Minister was not obliged to give information to the requesters. First of all, because the disclosure of the contract would harm the interests of a private company.

And we are left to answer several questions: Should not the Minister, who is the head of the state administration (and who is responsible by the law for several public registers of particular importance – that of the public procurements, the concessions, and the Access to Public Information Act), be the model of transparency and accountability to all administrations?

Or is it only the 150 to 500 euro procurements that would be really public?

Gergana Jouleva and Alexander Kashumov work for the Access to Information Project (AIP), Sofia, Bulgaria.

Footnotes

1 Under the Bulgarian legislation failure of public administration to decide on a matter within the prescribed time frames is considered a negative decision (refusal).

2 The Minister of State Administration reports annually on the implementation of APIA under art. 16 of the law.

16

UK's anti-terrorism measures fall short of European standards

Virginia Mantouvalou

It is not only the European Court of Human Rights that safeguards fundamental freedoms in the fight against terror. Various non-judicial organs of the Council of Europe (the organisation with the longest tradition in human rights protection at supranational level) recently scrutinised and severely criticised the detention conditions of foreign terrorism suspects in the United Kingdom as well as the country's new anti-terrorism legislation.

Over the last few years the Council of Europe introduced numerous initiatives in the effort to control State Parties' response to terrorism. The adoptions by the Committee of Ministers of the Guidelines on Human Rights and the Fight against Terrorism in 2002, and in their more recent 2005 version, were only the start of the organisation's comprehensive campaigns to guarantee human rights. The organisation's efforts to guarantee human rights have always been coupled by a clear recognition of the grave threat that terrorism poses to democratic, pluralistic societies with long traditions in the protection of fundamental freedoms. The UK was the keenest among the organisation's member states that introduced special measures after 9/11, thus derogating from the European Convention on Human Rights. No other country of the organisation, which now counts 46 member states, found it necessary to suspend any provision of the Convention, and this may be why the UK attracted special attention and was subject to scrutiny. The Anti-terrorism Crime and Security Act 2001, as well as the Prevention of Terrorism Act 2005, have raised serious concerns and have been criticised on a number of occasions. The most recent expressions of concern as to the legislation and its specific implementation are to be found in the Report of the Committee against Torture and that of the High Commissioner for Human Rights, Alvaro Gil-Robles.

The European Committee for the Prevention of Torture (CPT) is a non-judicial body of independent and impartial experts that monitors compliance with the 1987 European Convention on the Prevention of Torture and Inhuman or Degrading Treatment and Punishment. Its role is primarily preventive. A delegation of the Committee visited the United Kingdom in March 2004. The Committee's aim was to examine the treatment of international terrorism suspects, who were being detained under the Anti-Terrorism, Crime and Security Act 2001 (ATCSA), and to assess the developments after its previous visit in 2002. The findings of the delegation showed that detention conditions were far from appropriate, causing serious mental and physical suffering to the detainees.

The Committee visited persons who were held from 2002 in Belmarsh Prison, the Woodhill Prison and the Broadmoor Special Hospital. The detailed Report[1] that it adopted and the Response[2] of the UK Government were published in June 2005. Detainees' allegations as well as facts that the Committee itself established during the visit included the following: detainees suffered serious mental health and psychiatric problems, suffering from depression, symptoms of psychosis, post-traumatic stress disorder, distress, suspicion and ideas of suicide. The treatment they received from prison staff in Belmarsh gave rise to serious concerns on the part of the delegation that stressed that 'the risk of the situation getting out of hand is far from theoretical'. Allegations of ill treatment upon arrest, as well as whilst in detention were striking. One detainee, for instance, claimed that he was put in isolation by the prison's staff for a night, with no clothing on and with the ventilation system on, because he was praying loudly – an allegation that the authorities confirmed. The delegation found that prison staff frequently threatened detainees that they would be put in the 'intensive-care suite', used aggressive and abusive language and laughed with derision while watching prisoners through a camera. Moreover, certain detainees were subject to racist behaviour, and prison staff did not intervene. The Committee stressed that this treatment cannot be tolerated and is not to be sanctioned. Another patient was put in the Broadmoor Special Hospital. The Committee, the medical team of the hospital, as well as numerous other doctors, said that this is an inappropriate environment for someone in his condition. The delegation noted a profound lack of awareness of how to deal with someone who suffers severe post-traumatic stress disorder, bordering on psychosis. Detainees' past traumatic experiences were re-awakened due to the conditions of their detention.

More generally the Committee observed that the authorities were at a loss when they had to handle the indefinitely imprisoned ATCSA detainees. The unique conditions under which they were held, characterised mainly by the lack of a real prospect of release, resulted in serious physical and mental disorders which, from the delegation's view, could be said to amount to *inhuman and degrading treatment*. While the Committee, after its 2002 visit, anticipated that detainees would suffer such serious health problems and recommended that the authorities take appropriate action, the authorities did not offer the detainees the necessary support. The ATCSA detainees, the delegation of the Committee stressed, are subject to immigration rather than criminal legislation, and this special status had to be taken into account while they were held in prison. Their special status should be reflected in their detention conditions. They should be allowed to be involved in educational and intellectual activities, training and work, to pray and to practise their religion. They should also be offered special psychological and social support. The Committee also raised issues with respect to the right to notification of custody, access to a lawyer and access to a doctor which it considers to be fundamental rights and which it invited the authorities to address. The Report concludes with numerous recommendations to the UK authorities, calling upon them to guarantee effectively that those detained under the ATCSA are held in humane conditions, which will not have a damaging impact upon their physical and mental health.

The UK Government's response to the findings of the Committee had two parts. In the first part, it set out the new Prevention of Terrorism Act 2005, which, it claimed, would address the issues that were raised by the 14th December House of Lords decision on the compatibility of the ATCSA with the obligations under the European Convention on Human Rights. The Law Lords held in their judgment that the measures were, on the one hand, discriminatory as they only targeted foreign nationals and, on the other hand, disproportionate. Accordingly, in light of the new legislation, the Government said, it would be both citizens and non-citizens that would be held for terrorism-related activities. The suspects would not be imprisoned, as was the case with the 2001 Act, but be only subject to 'control orders'. All ATCSA detainees were, therefore, released from prison, and put under these new control orders. The second part of the Response took the findings of the delegation and addressed them in detail. The thrust of the Government's response was that, contrary to the Committee findings, detention conditions in

163

Belmarsh Prison and in the Broadmoor Special Hospital were not inhuman and degrading, and could not give rise to any issue under article 3 of the European Convention on Human Rights. Only a few of the allegations, the Government said, were substantiated, while most were unsubstantiated and for others there was insufficient evidence. It expressed, therefore, its satisfaction that detention conditions in UK prisons did not fall short of European standards.

The High Commissioner for Human Rights (an independent and impartial non-judicial institution within the Council of Europe) visited Edinburgh, Belfast and London in November 2004 and published a report on his visit in June 2005.[3] Alvaro Gil-Robles did not deal with the Anti-Terrorism Crime and Security Act 2001 specific provisions as the House of Lords had already held that the Act is incompatible with the European Convention on Human Rights before the Commissioner's report. The Commissioner welcomed the House of Lords ruling. The new Prevention of Terrorism Act, however, raised serious issues. According to the PTA 2005 the Secretary of State for Home Affairs can make control orders against individuals if he has reasonable grounds for suspecting them of being involved in terrorist related activities. The measures that the Act allows the Secretary of State to adopt include restrictions on work and other activities, on association, communication, movement, residence, and going as far as house arrest. The realisation that some of these measures may be contrary to the European Convention is evident in the legislation as the Act itself provides that for some of the measures derogation from the Convention will be necessary, without, however, stating which will be the measures that will require derogation and which will not.

Is the 2005 legislation compatible with the UK's international obligations? The Commissioner expressed considerable concern in his Report, and examined the compatibility of the new Act with, first, the protection of individual liberty, and, second, the right to a fair trial. Leaving aside the derogating control orders, as they had not been implemented before the report, and with the hope that they would not be considered necessary, Mr. Robles turned to the non-derogating control orders. The judiciary's involvement in their imposition would only be very limited, the Commissioner stressed, the procedural guarantees few, and certainly far from criminal proceedings' guarantees. Non-derogating control orders might amount to unlawful deprivation of liberty under article 5(1) of the

Convention. The question, therefore, whether a specific measure falls within the scope of the Convention and might require derogation should, the Commissioner recommended, be a matter for judicial scrutiny.

The right to a fair trial under article 6 of the European Convention on Human Rights also comes into play under the new Act, the Commissioner noted, as the control orders may be said to be criminal measures. The UK does not characterise these orders as *criminal*, and it is precisely because it does not initiate criminal proceedings against the suspects that *executive* control orders are adopted. This, however, cannot impede Courts from examining whether the orders are in fact 'criminal', despite the domestic classification, and require, as a result, the fair trial guarantees of the Convention. The control orders are brought for alleged involvement in suspected criminal acts, and are of a level of severity similar to that of a criminal penalty. The limited role that the Act affords the judiciary, furthermore, falls short of fair trial requirements with the proceedings being 'inherently one-sided'. The Courts cannot determine whether the specific charges are criminal, while equality of arms is not safeguarded, Mr. Robles explained. The Prevention of Terrorism Act allows, among others, the consideration of secret evidence and the participation of special advocates who cannot discuss the evidence with the suspects. What the new measures under the 2005 Act achieve, the Commissioner went on to state, is 'to substitute the ordinary criminal justice system with a parallel system run by the executive'. Two guarantees are therefore required so that the Act is compatible with the Convention. First, the Commissioner recommends judicial guarantees need to apply in the proceedings under the Act. Second, the legislation in question has to be subject to regular review by Parliament.

There is no doubt that terrorism poses a great danger to liberal democratic societies, which a democracy cannot easily address. However grave the threat of terrorism may be, though, it should not lead to compromises in the levels of tolerance and protection of fundamental rights as this might lead only to more polarisation and extremism. The UK legislation and its implementation are the 'real threat to the life of the nation' that international terrorism poses, as Lord Hoffman emphasised. Innocent victims of human rights abuses are not only those who are killed in terrorist attacks, but also those who are indefinitely detained in inhuman conditions without sufficient evidence and with no basic guarantees of a fair trial. This situation is to be avoided at any cost. The UK Government appears to be moving in the wrong direction, advancing all the more repressive strategies, while it is exactly under the present conditions that it should not give in to pressures for the adoption of anti-liberal repressive policies. International bodies, though, are there to monitor its actions. In an era where human rights protection has become one of the primary concerns of the international community, attempts to restrict liberties that are well established and crucial do not pass unquestioned. The Council of Europe has more than its influential Court to achieve its objectives. The European Committee for the Prevention of Torture and the Commissioner for Human Rights are two other organs that show that in difficult times and times of crisis, when Courts are put under pressure by the executive, there are other bodies that can complement and support their role. These bodies can protect a minority whose voice is weak and cannot be heard by majorities and their elected representatives. The UK Government, one of the founding members of the Council of Europe, with a long tradition in the protection of civil liberties, ought to take these Reports seriously into account and bring its policies in line with evolving European standards.

Virginia Mantouvalou holds an LLB (University of Athens) and an LLM (LSE). She is currently a PhD candidate and teaching assistant at the LSE, and a visiting lecturer at UCL and represents the Hellenic League of Human Rights in the European Civil Liberties Network.

Footnotes

1 Report to the Government of the UK on the visit carried out by the European Committee on the Prevention of Torture and Inhuman or Degrading Treatment or Punishment, CPT/Inf (2005) 10.

2 Response of the UK Government to the Report, CPT/Inf (2005) 11.

3 Report by the Commissioner for Human Rights on his visit to the United Kingdom, CommDH (2005) 6.